To further an understanding of regional history

THE GLEASON MEMORIAL FUND

has provided funds to print 700 copies of

GENESEE COUNTRY VILLAGE

for distribution to schools and libraries
throughout the Genesee Region.

The Genesee Country Museum was conceived and founded by John L. Wehle who from its inception in 1966 has served as Chairman of the Board of Trustees. "Jack" Wehle, a lifetime collector of sporting art, perceived that another art form — the work of regional carpenters, master builders, and housewrights — was fast disappearing from the landscape and with it was vanishing an important aspect of the Genesee Valley heritage. He proposed a museum village of selected examples of nineteenth-century Genesee country architecture. The buildings would be showcases in which the art of the cabinetmaker, the weaver, the potter and other artisans would be displayed in appropriate cultural context.

A rise above the Oatka Creek in a quiet corner of Monroe County, New York, was chosen for the museum site. Much of the land, once cleared and farmed, had reverted to the wild state which greeted the first settlers. Stone fences trailing through the rolling woodlands and anchoring the hedgerows remained as evidence of the frontier farming venture.

For ten years the founder and the museum director, architectural historian Stuart Bolger, guided a corps of carpenters and masons in turning the long-neglected land to new and useful purposes in the form of a recreated village. During the first decade of development some three dozen buildings of the style, type, and function found in the rural communities of western New York State were acquired and set down in the configuration of an early Genesee Country hamlet. Vintage farm structures were moved in and placed alongside the Village. With care and historical respect these buildings were restored.

In the meantime the curatorial staff undertook the quest for relevant artifacts with which to furnish and equip the renewed buildings. Opened to the public in 1976, the museum during its second decade doubled in size and content.

The two hundred acres occupied by the Museum buildings are surrounded by over a thousand acres of grain and corn fields, grasslands, ponds, and wetlands which furnish a rich habitat for game and wildfowl. The ongoing development of the Nature Center, another of the Museum's missions, affords opportunities for the public to observe the undisturbed flora and the unthreatened fauna within the preserve.

Complementing the emphasis which the Village places upon a narrow portion of the American experience, the Gallery of Sporting Art, as a further dimension of the museum program, offers a wide range of commentary on natural history, presented through the work of hundreds of internationally recognized artists and sculptors.

ISBN 0-931535-05-0 (Hard Cover)
ISBN 0-931535-06-9 (Soft Cover)
Library of Congress Catalog Card Number: 93-72617
© First Edition: 1985
© Second Edition: 1993
by Genesee Country Museum, Flint Hill Road, Mumford, New York 14511
All rights reserved.
No part of this book may be reproduced in any form
without written permission of Genesee Country Museum.
Printed in the USA by Flower City Printing, Inc., Rochester, New York 14612

The Genesee Country Museum is a not-for-profit institution chartered by the Board of Regents of the University of the State of New York for the education and enjoyment of the public.

GENESEE COUNTRY VILLAGE

SCENES OF TOWN & COUNTRY IN THE NINETEENTH CENTURY

By Stuart Bolger

The Genesee Country Museum, Mumford, New York

It was in country villages more than on isolated farms or in the few widely scattered cities that American society flourished during the Jeffersonian years. This was especially true in the Genesee Country where by the 1820s and 1830s some forty hamlets and villages were providing economic services and other community functions for the flood of settlers who were clearing and developing its rich lands. Each village had its special character and history, but all supplied urgent needs, nurturing a thriving homespun society rich with creative energies.

In an endeavor to visualize and interpret this bygone era, the Genesee Country Village has assembled authentic examples—functional buildings and artifacts of the period—from a score of area towns. It has not endeavored to recreate any specific village but to recapture and portray the character and atmosphere of the village era.

The Genesee Country villages were a product of their historic time, geographic place and population diversity. They differed in striking ways from the closely knit "covenanted" towns of colonial New England, initially comprised of a single congregation whose members cultivated the surrounding fields; they also differed from the plantation marts in the southern colonies where slaves and indentured servants performed services for absentee masters.

Except for a few major towns planned by the agents of land companies—Canandaigua by Oliver Phelps, Bath and Geneva by Charles Williamson, Batavia by the Holland Land Company, Rochester by a convergence of vigorous promoters—the Genesee villages were located and built by enterprising pioneers (some of them Yankees, some Yorkers, some from Pennsylvania or the South) who seized the opportunity to provide their fellow settlers with taverns, stores, mills, tanneries and smiths, as well as churches, libraries and academies to fit their varied tastes.

The newly opened territory, covered in large part by a virgin forest, seemed boundless to many, but it was conveniently held together and identified by the Genesee River and its broad and fertile valley. The Genesee, the longest north-flowing river in the United States (interrupted in its course by two series of spectacular waterfalls in the Letchworth and Rochester gorges) empties into Lake Ontario and might logically have tied the development of this area in with the British-controlled settlement of Canada. For several years in the 1790s that seemed a possibility, but the Seneca Indians, the largest and strongest of the six Iroquois nations, who for 300 years had occupied the Genesee, "Beautiful Valley" as they named it, finally reached agreement with the newly formed federal government for peaceful coexistence.

It is worth pausing for a brief look at the Senecas, for these prior inhabitants of the Genesee Country also lived in villages but with a distinctly different lifestyle. Theirs were stockaded settlements generally planted on hilltops for added security. They had a communal society, with several families' dwelling together in longhouses built of bark. Volumes have been written about their family and social patterns, but for our purpose the essential characteristic was their communal economy. Lacking a strong sense of private property, they were content with a self-sufficient reliance on communal gardens and the produce of their hunters. The latter had for decades supplied a surplus of furs to exchange for the white man's guns, powder, pots and blankets, and for supplies of rum. But when the fur trade was exhausted and their service as mercenaries was terminated with the return of peace, their only remaining surplus was in land. Their reluctant negotiations for the sale of vast tracts to three large land companies, preserving only limited reservations for permanent occupancy, opened the Genesee to settlement in the 1790s.

The pioneers who rushed in to clear and develop the new frontier were each hoping to improve his lot. They eagerly made down payments for coveted acres, and to make their titles good they had to produce and market a surplus of field and forest products. Theirs was to be a commercial, not a self-sufficient economy, and they turned to the villages for the assistance of merchants, craftsmen and professional men who collaborated in the formation of a vibrant homespun society, which proved to be a fertile parent of the urban-industrial society that replaced it after the mid-century.

Blake McKelvey
City Historian of Rochester, Emeritus

Genesee Country Museum - from an oil painting by J. L. Wehle, 1983.

THE RIVER

From a hill in Potter County, Pennsylvania, three small streams start off in different directions. One heads eastward via the Susquehanna system for the Atlantic Ocean, several hundred miles distant. Another begins an even longer passage down the Allegheny, Ohio, and Mississippi Rivers to the Gulf of Mexico.

The journey of the third, the Genesee, is short— 144 miles. The stream winds northward from the Allegheny plateau, cutting through the rugged upland of New York's Southern Tier, drops over a succession of cataracts, threads the long, deep, awesome gorge at Letchworth, then flows quietly among rolling hill country and between flanking alluvial flatlands. Along the way it is fed by numerous tributaries - the Canaseraga, Honeoye, Oatka, Black, and Red Creeks among them. Together these streams provided natural routes for pioneer traders through the Genesee heartlands.

Within the present city of Rochester the amplified Genesee plunges over the Niagara escarpment in three (originally four) spectacular waterfalls. These falls effectively interrupted trade on the upper river and made Rochester the terminus for logs and grain coming downstream—and at the same time supplied waterpower for Rochester's battery of gristmills and sawmills to convert the logs and grain into lumber and flour. After its final descent the river passes through another gorge and then spills into Lake Ontario. The river's irregular course bisects western New York State and provides natural boundaries for many of the townships into which the Genesee valley has been divided.

The course and character of the Genesee were determined by glacial events. The most dramatic effect of the retreating glaciers was to block the lower course of the river by deposits that prevented its original discharge through Irondequoit Bay, forcing it to carve a new outlet through the hills to the west, producing the present series of falls and the lower Genesee gorge. In addition, the receding ice sheet left behind rock-rubbish or glacial drift, an important ingredient of the fertile soil in the broad lower river valley.

Over untold millenia the scraped-over land gradually quickened and nurtured thick forest and lush grasslands. The lakes and streams of the region teemed with fish; the woodlands abounded with animals, great and small; the climate was temperate.

Native Americans to the south and west learned of this wondrous virgin hunting ground. "So came the wandering archaic Algonkian, battling for the region with Eskimoan peoples, and then other waves of Algonkian peoples, and still other waves until the land was old to man." (Arthur C. Parker in *The Natural Forces that Moulded the Genesee Country.)*

Later, also from the west, came people who called themselves "The Men of Men"—the Iroquois— tough, energetic, and ambitious. On their way east different tribes of these Iroquois travelled different routes. Some crossed the Detroit River, circling above Lake Erie and Lake Ontario; of these the Wyandot-Hurons settled down north of the lower Great Lakes and the St. Lawrence River. Others— the Cayugas, the Mohawks, and the Oneidas— moved on, crossing the St. Lawrence and sweeping down to occupy what is now central New York State. There they would come in contact with their kinsmen, the Onondagas, who had migrated more directly from the Ohio region toward the rising sun.

In 1796 Louis Philippe of France, the 23-year-old Duc d'Orleans, arrived in Philadelphia, followed by his younger brothers, the Duc de Montpensier and the Duc de Beaujolais. The three were exiled after their father was guillotined by the Directory during the French Revolution. On a visit to George Washington at Mt. Vernon, the young men announced their intention of seeing the interior of America. Crossing the Appalachians, they journeyed up the Ohio into the Genesee Country.

At Canandaigua they were greeted by Thomas Morris, son of financier and land speculator Robert Morris. Young Morris guided them to the Genesee Falls; they stayed the night with pioneer Orringh Stone in his small house at the junction of two Indian trails, in present day Brighton, just south of Rochester.

This view, painted by the Duc de Beaujolais, of the travelers enjoying the prospect from the east bank below the cataract, is the earliest known oil painting of the falls. The striking detail, the great vertical slabs of rock that border the falls, reveals that the Duc could only have made a rough sketch of the falls while at the site and later in Philadelphia made a painting from that sketch, forgetful of the layers of rock strata that line the gorge.

In 1839, after he had been crowned King of France, Louis Philippe wrote that his three year stay in America "had a great influence on my political opinions and on my judgement of the course of human affairs."

Upper falls of the Genesee River at the site of modern Rochester.

THE IROQUOIS

The Senecas also traveled northward, some along the Ohio and Allegheny rivers, others along the southern shore of Lake Erie. Reaching the fair land of the northward flowing river they forced aside the less warlike Algonkians and claimed the territory as their own. They bestowed upon the river a name meaning "Pleasant Valley" - "Gen-nis-he-y." In time the whole region would become known as "Genesee Country."

About the time explorers from Europe were probing the east coast of North America, the Senecas, the Onondagas, the Cayugas, the Oneidas, and the Mohawks formed the Iroquois Confederacy. Hiawatha, an Onondaga chief, was a major force in forming the Confederacy. Other tribes of Iroquois, among them the powerful Hurons, did not join.

The Senecas were designated "Keepers of the Western Door;" the Mohawks "Keepers of the Eastern Door." Between these portals was the "Long House," the term the Iroquois symbolically applied to their domain, a reference to their elongated, bark-covered multi-family dwellings. For nearly two centuries the Confederacy held its ground - from the Hudson River valley to the lower Great Lakes. For the powerful tribes who had pushed up from the Ohio and Mississippi it had been "a journey toward dawn and it led to a golden age."

Within the forests of their vast territory the Iroquois lived in scattered villages, clearing enough land to cultivate corn, pumpkins, squash, and tobacco. While the women planted and harvested their crops, picked apples and peaches from their orchards, and gathered wild fruit and berries, the braves hunted and fished and provided protection. Over all and within all living things, the Iroquois believed, was their creator, for whose favor they applied through seasonal festivals of thanksgiving.

Colonel King Hendrick in the characteristic war paint of an Iroquois chieftain, circa 1775. The marks above the ear and under the eyes signify "I hear all; I see all." The absence of paint near the mouth means "I am silent."

6

THE EUROPEANS

The golden age of the Iroquois was doomed when the ancient rivalry between England and France shifted to this side of the Atlantic, setting the stage for a century-long struggle between the European powers for supremacy over the lands where the Indians held tenure. At stake for the contending foreigners were sovereignty over the seemingly endless virgin territories of North America and the more immediate profits from the fur trade. The stakes for the Indians: survival.

North of the St. Lawrence, the Hurons allied with the French; to the south, the Hurons' old rivals, the Iroquois, leaned to the British. On both sides the native Americans were courted with guns and powder; knives, axes, and kettles of metal; beads and liquor.

In 1687 the Governor of New France, the Marquis de Denonville, annoyed by Iroquois interception of fur shipments destined for the French markets, led his troops across Lake Ontario and established a beachhead in Seneca territory. The French were accompanied by their Indian allies, among them a number of Hurons eager for Iroquois scalps. After destroying a large Seneca stronghold near present-day Victor, New York, and laying waste a number of nearby Indian villages, Denonville withdrew, satisfied he had chastised and humiliated the Iroquois.

In spite of the localized havoc left in its wake, the Marquis' expedition only increased the enmity of the Iroquois. When the showdown came between England and France the Iroquois helped the British take the French fortress at Niagara and lent occasional aid whenever it suited them. The Treaty of Paris in 1763 ended both the war and the French adventure in North America as "half a continent changed hands at the scratch of a pen."

A grateful King George III rewarded the opportunistic Iroquois by prohibiting further encroachment on Indian lands west of the Appalachian Mountains. This blocking of westward expansion delayed the opening of the Genesee Country as well as the yet unsettled regions beyond the mountain chain. The ban also had the unsuspected result of knitting together more tightly the thirteen colonies as they moved inexorably toward open rebellion.

Joseph Brant (Thayendorogea), a Mohawk chieftain serving under Sir William Johnson and Colonel Guy Johnson, fought on the side of the British in the French and Indian War and during the Revolutionary War.

A devout Christian who in more peaceful days translated The Book of Common Prayer into the Mohawk tongue, Brant attempted to prevent the mistreatment of the captured foes in the Tory and Indian raids on the Mohawk Valley settlements.

Following the war Brant contended for the rights of the hapless Iroquois. In this 1786 portrait Gilbert Stuart captures the Mohawk chief in full regalia.

When the Revolutionary War broke out the British found the Iroquois reluctant to become involved. "The determination of the Six Nations," said 'Little Abraham', a Mohawk spokesman, "is not to take any part; but as it is a family affair to sit still and see you fight it out." Eventually, the Mohawks, the Senecas, the Onondagas, and the Cayugas were persuaded by Sir William Johnson, long-time friend of the Indians, to participate in the Tory-led bloody raids upon the frontier settlements. By accommodating the British in these terrorist attacks, the ill-advised Indians invited a fateful invasion of their homeland. In 1779 General of the Army George Washington dispatched Major General John Sullivan with a third of the Continental Army to ravage the territory of the Iroquois. "The immediate object," instructed Washington, "is the total destruction of the settlements of the Six Nations and the capture of as many persons as possible."

Iroquois scouts, peering down from the wooded hillsides, saw the strung-out columns of the advancing Continentals as "a long blue snake." Near Newtown (Elmira) the combined Tory and Indian forces fortified a position between the hills and the Chemung River and awaited the invaders. On a summer afternoon Sullivan's forewarned and well-deployed regulars outflanked the fortifications and gained an easy victory.

The Continental Army of nearly four thousand men then marched unopposed into the Genesee Country ruining whatever of the "longhouse" lay in its path. The empty villages of the Senecas and Cayugas were burned, the golden corn fields and the orchards laden with ripening fruit were cut down, and stored provisions were taken or destroyed.

After crossing the Genesee River, Sullivan found that the enemy warriors together with refugee families from the abandoned villages had hurried toward the British base at Niagara. Judging his own supplies inadequate to prolong the chase, the general headed his troops homeward.

As they passed through the Genesee Valley and the Finger Lakes on the long trek back, Sullivan's men had time to appraise the verdant, now deserted, landscape. They were impressed. "The most beautiful I have ever seen," said one of the officers of the land of the Genesee Country. Some of Sullivan's victorious soldiers would one day return to have a go at the wilderness, to build new homes among the ashes of the burned-out longhouses.

Superimposed on this 1771 map of the Iroquois homeland ("the Country of the VI. Nations") are the routes taken by Sullivan and Clinton in their mission to overrun and destroy the Indian settlements. The advance is shown in blue, the return in red.

E.B. O'CALLAGHAN'S *Documentary History of the State of New York,* **1851.**

In 1779 General John Sullivan, moving up from eastern Pennsylvania and reinforced by General James Clinton coming down from the Mohawk Valley, effectively forced the Iroquois and their Tory allies from the Genesee Country.

THE LAST DAYS OF THE LONGHOUSE

In the treaty that concluded the Revolutionary War, Britain recognized the Mississippi River as the western boundary of the "free, independent, and sovereign states." A corner of that vast, varied, and undeveloped domain received almost immediate attention—the Genesee Country, which stretched from the Finger Lakes to the lower Great Lakes. The beauty and bounty acclaimed by Sullivan's veterans was also reported by British travelers riding through on their way to the Niagara frontier. Soon word on the Genesee Country was out and land speculators were ready to move in.

But there were obstacles impeding the white men's takeover of the Iroquois' old hunting grounds. Though many Americans believed the Indian lands should be forfeit and confiscated, President Washington upheld the Indians' claim to their ancestral territory. Indian land, said Washington, could be obtained only through treaty and purchase. Disposition of Genesee Country land was further snarled by conflicting claims of Massachusetts and New York over jurisdiction. Finally the dispute was settled. Massachusetts was awarded the right of "preemption" (the right to negotiate with the Indians for the purchase of the land); thereafter New York would have political jurisdiction.

By 1793 Massachusetts had sold off its preemption rights to land companies and speculators who through hard bargaining and a series of treaties were able to buy out the Iroquois. Except for eleven Indian reserves in the Genesee Country, all of western New York State was available for the purposes of the white men by the beginning of the nineteenth century.

There were various marketing methods and patterns of settlement in the opening of the Genesee Country. Massachusetts developer Oliver Phelps established Canandaigua not only as headquarters for the Phelps and Gorham Company but also as a center where merchants and tradesmen could attend to the needs of the surrounding farming community. In laying out the townships in his land holdings, Phelps instructed his surveyors to designate likely spots for other village centers. His theory—that given a town center, settlers would surround it with prosperous farms—did not work out in practice, resulting in serious financial problems for his land company.

The six million acres of the Genesee Country — all the New York State land west of the "New Pre-emption Line" — are shown as divided after the completion of Robert Morris's sale of over three million acres to the Holland Land Company in 1793. The map, however, does not reflect the holdings of the Pulteney Associates who acquired all but two townships of the area identified here as the Phelps and Gorham Purchase. Thirteen western New York State counties and portions of two others now lie within the old Genesee Country.

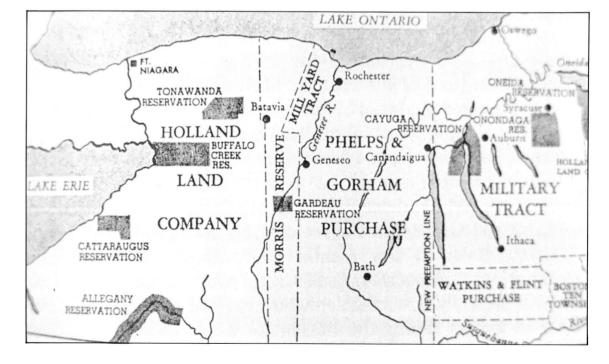

THE LAND AGENTS

A more flamboyant approach was used by Captain Charles Williamson, agent for the British based Pulteney Associates. Sir William Pulteney had acquired most of the unsold lands of the Phelps and Gorham Purchase from Robert Morris, the Philadelphia financier. A former British army officer, Williamson's approach to attracting settlers has been termed the "hot house" method. He built villages— Sodus, Lyons, Geneva, Williamsburg, and Bath—and he also built roads. He had his men hack out a road from central Pennsylvania through the wilderness, passing through his headquarters town of Bath and on into the heart of the Genesee Country.

At Bath, in short order, his workmen cleared over a thousand forested acres, built inns, a theatre, a fairgrounds, and a racetrack. In 1796, when there were only a few thousand inhabitants in all of the Genesee Country, over three thousand curious visitors were attracted to this master promoter's month-long fair and festival in the wilds of western New York. They followed guides Williamson had sent out to meet them in Montreal, New York City, Philadelphia, Baltimore and Richmond, and other cities along the eastern seaboard.

Alarmed by Williamson's extravagance and disappointing sales record, his employers replaced him with an agent less visionary and more practical. But the discharged Scotsman had done more to encourage the pioneer, to fan the fame of the Genesee Country and to advance its settlement than any other steward.

A similar attachment to the land and concern for the pioneer farmers who came to work it was shown by James Wadsworth, sent out from Connecticut to manage his family's interest in the Genesee Country and to act as agent for a number of absentee owners. The young Wadsworth initiated informational "Genesee Meetings" throughout New England at which he spoke and distributed handbills describing the excellent opportunities awaiting in western New York. Wadsworth's terms for buying land were liberal and flexible. He accepted farmland in New England in exchange for raw land in the Genesee Country. By introducing a tenant system, Wadsworth made it possible for poor settlers to make a living by farming. He made oxen available to help the pioneers clear the land; provided potash kettles so they could make a cash "crop" out of wood ashes; and, following the example of Williamson, accepted payment in kind from the hard-pressed pioneer.

Joseph Ellicott, agent for the Dutch investors in the Holland Land Company, was initially more conservative than any of the other agents, looking for private enterprise to provide mills and stores and for the government to build the roads. As his policy became more liberal he helped finance the construction of roads, mills, and even set aside land for schools and churches.

Though their policies differed, land agents in the Genesee Country shared a common goal: to sell land to individual farmers—to get the territory settled and improved. In 1818 Ellicott reported to his supervisors that the prime land of the Holland Land Company had been "taken up." The following year James Wadsworth noted that most of the land in his region was "under improvement." The tracts which the agents reserved for themselves or for their companies appreciated in value as the adjacent areas were improved by the toil of the pioneer farmers.

LAND OFFICE BUSINESS

The success the Wadsworths enjoyed in their Genesee Country real estate undertakings was not matched by some of the other large-scale speculators in wild New York lands. Among the long-range losers were Oliver Phelps, his partner Nathaniel Gorham, and his old wartime friend, Philadelphia banker, Robert Morris.

In 1789 Oliver Phelps established the first land office in the United States — in a log building at Canandaigua. Sales lagged and cash returns were not sufficient to meet the Phelps and Gorham group's 300,000 pound sterling indebtedness.

A bail-out came with the entry of Robert Morris into the contest for western New York State land. Morris bought rights to all the unsold portions of the original Phelps and Gorham Purchase. But despite his spectacularly profitable deals in unloading two million acres east of the Genesee River to the Pulteney Associates and over three million more acres west of the river to the Holland Land Company, Morris's debts mounted faster than his income. The financial savior of the Continental Army, as General George Washington termed him, could not save himself.

A sheriff's sale in 1799 deprived Robert Morris of what was left of his special reserve of 500,000 lush areas in the Genesee Valley. His debts landed him in the Walnut Street prison in Philadelphia.

Land speculation was a hazardous business. Absentee landlords were soon disenchanted when their expectations for quick profits from wholesaling large tracts to land-hungry investors proved wishful.

And The Pulteney Associates were growing wary of Resident-Agent Capt. Charles Williamson's expense accounts for travel and entertainment and costly expenditures for road building and improvements at his headquarters in Bath — he had built a large new house to please his wife and a new land office to please himself and his clerks.

Williamson recognized that to boost sluggish sales he would have to sell modest parcels to individual farmers. To expedite such sales Williamson enlisted sub-agents to establish offices in other regions of his territory and to set about making "improvements." But time ran out on the free-wheeling Resident-Agent. Sir William Pulteney in London replaced Williamson with a more conservative and practical promoter, Robert Troup.

One of Williamson's sub-agents (who was retained by Troup), was 24-year-old Henry Towar. By 1794 he had built a gristmill, sawmill and a clothiery (for carding and dressing spun wool) on the Canandaigua Lake outlet — and raised a log house for his land office.

First known simply as Towar's Mills, the settlement was renamed Alloway, after Towar's birthplace in Alloa, a town near Edinburgh, Scotland. (Poet Robert Burns was also born in Alloa).

When Towar arrived in Alloway, unimproved land was selling for two dollars an acre and money was scarce. Payments could be made in wheat delivered to the gristmill. The best grain was saved for the distillery which shrewd Henry Towar had erected near the gristmill; the second best went for flour and feed.

This enterprising young agent also built an ashery where wood ashes bought from farmers were refined to form pearlash, a very marketable industrial product.

With help from his brothers and sons, Henry Towar prospered in Alloway. He built a handsome house. His village, strategically located on the main road connecting Sodus Bay on Lake Ontario with Geneva on Seneca Lake, seemed destined for importance. But the Erie Canal and later the railroad bypassed Alloway, which subsided into a quiet rural hamlet.

Captain and Mrs. Henry Towar. (Courtesy of Wayne County Historical Society)

When Henry Towar acquired a large area of "unimproved" land near Alloway he needed help to clear it and work it. One of his farm workers later wrote: "Mr. Towar came to Bath to hire some slaves and I was one of the three he hired… The Towars cleared a great number of acres during the first year. He never flogged me but treated me kindly. He did a heavy business in the mill, store and distillery."

In 1808 when the New York State law of manumission was enacted and Towar freed his slaves, they chose to remain with him.

Toward the end of his active career Captain Towar, whose first office had been a log structure, erected a smart little Greek Revival building. When its days as a land office ended it served as a doctor's office, a butcher shop, and a filling station.

It has lately reassumed its first purpose and been provided with the tools of Captain Towar's trade— maps, charts, ledgers, a letter press, a safe and surveying instruments.

A Speculator Founds a City

Panic gripped the country in the spring of 1837 as the nation's banks, which had called in their loans, closed their doors. Henry Towar, who had borrowed heavily to maintain cash flow in his many enterprises, was wiped out. His brothers and sons left Alloway to seek their fortunes elsewhere.

The 1837 panic also made matters worse for settlers already struggling with the unfriendly terrain in portions of the Holland Purchase. After twenty years as Resident-Agent for the Holland Land Company, Joseph Ellicott was dismissed.

With Ellicott's departure the Dutch bankers initiated stricter policies. When these aggressive absentee landlords pressed the settlers for payments of accumulated debts they only succeeded in earning the increased enmity of their debtors. In 1835 a mob of enraged farmers sacked the office of the company agent, scattering its records. Many settlers refused to pay their debts to "foreign interests" and the Holland Land Company was forced to close their offices and sell out their holdings to American bank interests.

Prospects for rural prosperity seemed more promising in lands lying east of the Holland Land Purchase. This view was presented to three well-heeled gentlemen from the South who were being shown about the lower Genesee Valley by the Pulteney Associates' Resident-Agent Captain Charles Williamson, shortly before being relieved of his post.

One of the three men, Col. Nathaniel Rochester, recalled that trip in his autobiography:

In September, 1800, Major Carroll, Colonel Fitzhugh, Colonel Hilton and I visited the Genesee Country in western New York. Carroll and Fitzhugh purchased 12,000 acres of land, where they now reside. I purchased 400 acres adjoining their land; also 155 acres at Dansville…

In 1803 on a follow-up trip to look after their interests in the Genesee Country, Resident-Agent Robert Troup showed them the Genesee Falls where they saw the ruins of Indian Ebenezer Allan's primitive mills. (Allan had been given the site along the west side of the river in 1789 by Phelps and Gorham for his aid in their negotiations with the Iroquois). The southern gentlemen bought the Allan mill tract of 100 acres for $17.50 per acre. (The same year President Thomas Jefferson bought the Louisiana Territory for 15 million dollars – about two cents an acre).

Col. Rochester, a manufacturer and mill-man, recognized the power potential of the series of waterfalls. It would be he who would one day return to the Falls to found a city. But he did not leave his comfortable circumstances in Hagerstown, Maryland until 1810, when the inhabitants of the village bid a tearful farewell to the leading citizen.

The perilous 275-mile journey north through almost impassable mountains took three weeks. The Colonel on horseback led a procession of carriages bearing the women of the household and the younger children; three great "Conestoga" wagons with household goods and his ten slaves; and some of his neighbors who came along to help. The Colonel moved north, he said, "to escape the influence of slavery, to set his slaves free, and to rear his family in a free state."

Once settled in Dansville where he had purchased most of the water rights on Canaseraga Creek Col. Rochester erected a large paper mill and a gristmill. In the meantime he began to survey the 100 acre tract at the falls of the Genesee River, 45 miles to the north. Looking on, James Wadsworth wrote to Robert Troup, "I wish that tract of 100 acres could be purchased of the Maryland gentleman. The bridge and the mill-seat render it very valuable indeed."

Advertisement which appeared in Canandaigua newspaper as Col. Rochester prepared to move from Dansville. (Courtesy of City Historian's Office)

Col. Nathaniel Rochester

William Scott, an early resident of Dansville, described his meeting with Col. Rochester at a wayside tavern when the latter was returning from one of his visits to the Falls:

> I see him now riding up to the door, seated firmly on a small pacing mare, and carrying his surveyor's chain and compass strapped to the saddle. After a well-cooked meal, supper, to which our sharp appetites did full justice, we were shown to a room in the garret containing one bed. We occupied it together, though it was long before sleep visited us, for Colonel Rochester was full of flattering prospects at the Falls. "The place must become an important business point," said he and I expressed regret he had spent so much time and means in Dansville instead of going to the Falls at once… During the conversation I remarked that the name the "Falls" was good enough then, but added "of course you will find a more fitting name as the place increases." "Ah," said he, "I have already thought of that, and have decided to give it my family name," and that was the first time I ever heard the word "Rochester" applied to the present prosperous city.

After five years in Dansville, Col. Rochester moved to a large farm at East Bloomfield, and continued his work laying out the Village of Rochester.

In 1818 Col. Rochester and his family of 12 children finally moved near the Falls into a house with a large garden and grounds sloping down to the river. In 1824 he erected a brick house on higher ground where he resided the rest of his life — "venerated and beloved," wrote City Historian Edward Foreman in 1934, "he sacrificed personal gain in the interests of his village and died a relatively poor man."

Col. Nathaniel Rochester by John James Audubon. (Courtesy of Rochester Memorial Art Gallery)

Col. Rochester's Dansville plank house, now at Genesee Country Village, was bought by the Colonel from David Scholl (Captain Williamson's millwright) who is believed to have built it around 1795. Evidence revealed during its 1989 restoration suggests it may have had a dependent structure — in which case the Colonel's large family and the contents of three "Conestoga" wagons would have been less crowded.

THE PIONEERS

They came from the east and they came from the south. They were farmers from Connecticut and Massachusetts who had had enough of the tired soils and rocky hillsides and had heard or read about the fruitful Genesee Country. They were Pennsylvanians trailing up the Susquehanna, beckoned by reports of good cheap land beyond its headwaters.

They were tradesmen and mechanics seeking to better themselves. They were ambitious physicians' apprentices and lawyers' clerks anxious to hang out their shingles and build up their own practices.

There were those who saw their main chance in the need for stores and taverns in the new land. Millers viewed the many full-flowing streams as locations for profitable gristmills and sawmills. And there were entrepreneurs whose interest lay in the waterfalls of the Genesee River as bases for large-scale industrial development.

Some of these aspiring entrants would succeed. Some would be disappointed or become discouraged and turn back. Some would be struck down by "Genesee Fever," a form of malaria prevalent in the low-lying areas. Some would feel crowded as the Genesee Country began to fill, and they would pack up and move on to Ohio or Michigan.

But by far the greatest number were men who had come to stay—to own land, to clear it, and work it, and raise a family. It was they who with their worldly goods made the long haul to the Genesee Country, sought out the land agent, made a choice from the unsold parcels, negotiated the terms of sale, and began to tame the wilderness.

THE PIONEER SETTLER UPON THE HOLLAND PURCHASE, AND HIS PROGRESS.

The following excerpts of the progress of a settler in the Genesee Country—from his first encounter with the new environment to his comfortable situation forty five years later—are from Orsamus Turner's *Pioneer History of the Holland Land Purchase.*

"...He has taken possession of his new home. The oxen that are browsing, with the cow and three sheep; the two pigs and three fowls that his young wife is feeding from her folded apron; these, with a bed, two chairs, a pot and a kettle, and a few other indispensable articles for house keeping, few and scanty altogether, as may be supposed, for all were brought in upon that ox sled, through an underbrushed woods road; these constitute the bulk of his worldly wealth...

"...Miles and miles off, through the dense forest, is his nearest neighbor. Those trees are to be felled and cleared away, fences are to be made; here in this rugged spot, he is to carve out his fortunes and against what odds!..."

SECOND SKETCH OF THE PIONEER

"It is Summer. The pioneer has chopped down a few acres, enclosed them with a rail fence in front, and a brush fence on the sides and in the rear.

"Around the house he has a small spot cleared of the timber sufficient for a garden; but upon most of the opening he has made, he has only burned the brush, and corn, potatoes, beans, pumpkins, are growing among the logs. He has got a stick chimney added to his house.

"In the background of the picture, a logging bee is in progress; his scattered pioneer neighbors, that have been locating about him during the winter and spring, have come to join hands with him for a day, and in their turns, each of them will enjoy a similar benefit.

"His wife has become a mother, and with her first born in her arms, she is out, looking to the plants she has been rearing upon some rude mounds raised with her own hands."

THIRD SKETCH OF THE PIONEER

"It is Summer. Ten years have passed; our pioneer adventurer, it will be seen at the first glance, has not been idle; thirty or forty acres are cleared and enclosed.

"Various crops are growing, and the whole premises begin to have the appearance of careful management, of thrift, comfort, and even plenty.

"The pioneer has made a small payment upon his land, and got his 'article' renewed. He has put up a comfortable block house, but has had too much reverence for his primitive dwelling to remove it. He has a neat framed barn, surrounded by a picket fence. His stock is increased as may be seen, by a look off into the fields."

In a fourth and final sketch Turner's pioneer is "...prosperous in the midst of prosperity...honored and venerated, for his are the peaceful triumphs of early, bold enterprise...and long years of patient, persevering industry..." Such a comfortable situation did indeed reward large numbers of Genesee Country settlers.

THE PIONEER'S CABIN

While Turner's picturesque ("fancy," as Turner himself admitted) descriptions cannot be taken literally, they do suggest the typical and ceaseless effort required to overcome hardships facing the first generation of farmers in the Genesee Country.

A newspaper editor, Turner was a tireless compiler of reminiscences of those who had been part of the pioneering process. He himself had been a witness to the unfolding events.

And so had his artist, Ebenezer Mix. It is fitting that Mix presents the pioneer poised on his new land with his three closest companions: his wife, his cabin, and his axe. Without a house he would not long keep a wife. Without his axe he could not have built the house. Though the plow is a familiar symbol identifying agriculture, the axe was the one indispensable tool for the Genesee Country settler. He would some day walk behind a plow, but first he must swing his axe.

Passing through the Genesee Country on his way to the Niagara frontier, one traveler recalled that he was seldom out of earshot of the sound of axe biting into wood. In praise of the pioneer's axe Ulysses Hedrick in his *History of Agriculture in the State of New York* noted: "No other implement used by the pioneers in forest regions can compare in usefulness to the keen-edged, shining, trenchant American axe, skillfully hung on its helve of American hickory, and efficiently swung by corneous-handed American sons of toil in carving farms from the wilderness."

A man by himself might in a year chop down ten acres of Genesee Country virgin woodland. He would need help to clear away the felled logs—a team of oxen to drag them off or a number of neighbors to roll them aside. (He would have ample opportunity to return this as well as other future favors.) Then with little further preparation he could sow corn.

Logs not needed to build his cabin and some rude shelter for any livestock he possessed could be burned to give the settler one of his few cash crops— wood ashes. These he could leach, boil down in a large iron kettle and evaporate to form cakes of "black salts" or potash. Potash was in demand for bleaching, for the manufacture of glass, soap and medicine, as well as for a number of other commercial purposes. A ton of potash might bring as much as $200—a tidy sum alongside the eight or ten dollars a month a day laborer could expect to earn. Cash from his sales of potash would enable the settler to hire a laborer to help clear another ten acres of woodland, providing more room between the stumps to sow some grain and yielding potentially another ton of potash.

With a snug cabin, enough plain food for his family, some winter feed for his livestock, and a little cash to buy the essentials he could not himself produce, the pioneer farmer in the Genesee Country had made a modest beginning.

Contemporary accounts and inventories of similar cabins document the simple rude furnishings with which the cabin has been provided. Open hearth cooking and other food preparations are demonstrated daily in the Pioneer's Cabin during the Museum season.

On the lea of Flint Hill, just below the Village, are eight structures serving the needs of the pioneer farm family. The squared oak timbers on the one-room log cabin were laid up in 1806 by Nicholas Hetchler who first settled in the Genesee Country in 1787. Dovetail joints where the timbers overlap at the corners are typical of log house construction in Hetchler's native southern Pennsylvania.

A portion of one wall of solid stone masonry which provides a fireproof back for the clay fire hearth is characteristic of other early log cabins in the Genesee, as is the clay-lined wooden chimney.

The cabin was presented to the Museum by Arthur Burns whose family had occupied it for nearly a century in its original location just outside the nearby village of Scottsville. The excellent condition of the logs results from their long confinement within either frame additions to the cabin or clapboards applied to the exposed exterior walls.

Pioneer's cabin, c. 1810, from near Scottsville, New York.

THE PIONEER'S BARN

If the settler was fortunate enough to keep a milk cow, his family could enjoy dairy products and the cow could enjoy herself browsing in the brush and woods—until better pasturage could be developed. Swine could also get along rooting around in the forest; and a cooperative sow, given the chance, could provide the frontier family with fresh pork. Chickens could scratch around the clearing for enough to keep alive and to produce — by today's standards — a small quota of small eggs.

The pioneer farmer occasionally enhanced his meager menu with rabbit, squirrel, and other small game and, less frequently, with venison or wild turkey—depending always upon the conditions of his immediate environment. Even the Iroquois, expert hunters as they were, sometimes returned from the hunt with no deer in tow.

And the pioneer farmer had come to the Genesee Country to farm, not to hunt. He was too busy with the main task of removing the forest to spend much time roaming it in search of something for the table or the pot. He was more concerned with guarding against the wolves, bears, foxes and wild cats preying upon his precious livestock and the raccoons, woodchucks, squirrels, and crows working over his few crops.

What the pioneer wanted and needed most was a proper barn. As he enlarged his clearing so that he could sow more seed he also added simple structures to better protect his livestock from the extremes of the Genesee Country weather (as well as from the wild beasts of the surrounding forest). A log barn, which with a little help he could roll up as he had his cabin, would suffice temporarily. But a timber-framed barn with board siding was the real thing. Cash or credit, sawmills, neighbors, and know-how could set things right.

The main members of the framed barn were square-hewn from straight logs, usually hardwood. On the ground the posts and beams were joined together by mortice and tenon and pegs to form braced framed sections called 'bents'. Then it was time for the other settlers who had assembled for the purpose to raise the 'bents', pushing and tugging them up into a vertical stance. When the 'bents' had been tied together with horizontal members—"plates" and "girts"—the barn raising was finished

Then was the long-awaited moment for the women to bring forth food prepared for the event and the men to break out the cider and whiskey. Upon the stout timber framework the rafters— usually poles—were set. Roof boards were stretched across them, and upon these, row after row of shingles split from white pine or cedar were nailed into place. Wide boards from the sawmill were nailed vertically on the sides and ends, and after the doors were hung and the interior arrangements were completed the pioneer had a suitable place to quarter his animals, to thresh his grain, to store his hay, and to tinker on bad days. If without a house the pioneer could not keep a wife, without a barn he could hardly keep a farm in the Genesee Country.

Some early settlers kept a few sheep to provide wool for homespun clothing.

The wide central passageway of the pioneer's barn was called the "wagon" or "threshing" floor. Wagons piled high with hay were drawn alongside the animal stalls for unloading the hay onto the overhead mows.

After wheat harvest the sheaves were spread out upon the threshing floor to be trodden by unshod oxen or horses, or beaten by flails to separate the grain from the stalks. The straw was then raked away. Next, the remaining grain and chaff were "winnowed." The big doors at each end of the threshing floor were opened to set up a current of air. The farmer, filling his wooden winnowing tray or shallow winnowing basket with the grain and chaff, poured or tossed the mixture to let the breeze blow away the lighter chaff; the heavier grain dripping to the floor.

Some barns were built with "swing beams," huge squared timbers which spanned the entire width of the barn, carrying the heavy lofts without any intermediate support. On the unobstructed threshing floor, then, a horse could move in a wide circle, pulling a "groundhog thresher," a log with pegs driven into it and pivoted from a temporary central post. As the pegged log rolled across the spread out sheaves, the farmer kept turning the stalks and raking off the straw.

Circa 1820 barn built by a Connecticut Yankee in Ontario County, moved to the Pioneer Farmstead in 1985.

THE CROPS

Corn, the most important of the Indians' crops, was also the first reliable cereal crop the pioneer could produce in the rough conditions of nearly cleared land. The cultivation of corn and the knowledge of its many uses had been learned from the Indians by the first settlers to arrive in America. But the sweet corn grown by the Iroquois, as opposed to the Yankees' flint corn, was not known until Sullivan's soldiers came upon it ripening in the fields or dried and stored for times when other food was scarce. The Indians used corn meal, made by pounding dried corn in a wooden or stone mortar, mixed with meat in their mush and also baked as unleavened bread. So, following their example, did the hungry pioneer.

But a corn crop, however important, did not a Genesee Country farmer make. The pioneer soon discovered the fertile soil of the lower Genesee was admirably suited to the cultivation of wheat, although somewhat more preparation of the ground was required for wheat than for corn. In readying his new land for planting wheat the landsman, as one observer characterized the scene, steered around the stumps like a helmsman guiding his craft through an ice field. And from among his ten acres of stumps the pioneer would harvest—in the spring if was winter wheat and in late summer if it was spring wheat—150 bushels of marketable grain. One day the Genesee valley would be called the "Granary of the East"—but that salubrious time lay down roads not yet built.

In his description of the plants raised by the pioneer's wife Orsamus Turner fails to mention any vegetables; but in a paper discussing the history of vegetable gardening in the United States, Robert Becker of the New York Agricultural Experimental Station in Geneva, New York, lists the following possibilities: "Some turnips, a few cabbages, a row or two of beans, and a couple of hills of cucumbers probably comprised the average (pioneer's) garden. Wild greens were collected, especially in the early spring, and a small plot of peas was sown for winter use. Pumpkin seeds were planted here and there among the hills of corn." Becker also mentions potatoes and onions as likely additions to the list.

For the first few years it was a question of survival for many of the Genesee Countrymen. To break away from subsistence farming would be tough, although that assuredly was the hope and expectation of every man toiling in his clearing and the wish and dream of every woman bent with burdens about and around the cabin. Better times for the pioneer farmer in the Genesee Country would await better means of transport and the immigration of larger numbers of settlers in non-agricultural pursuits to populate the villages with consumers of farm products.

Like Nicholas Hetchler, whose one-story log cabin anchors the Pioneer's farmstead, Martin Kieffer moved from a settled area of southern Pennsylvania to carve a farm in the Genesee Country wilderness. And like Hetchler he built his dwelling of logs, using the same dovetail-like joints favored by the Germans in Pennsylvania.

But Kieffer's Place is a house, not a cabin. It contains eight rooms; its regularly spaced window and door openings form a symmetrical facade; and an enclosed stairway opposite the front entrance leads to the second floor.

At an early date lath and plaster were applied to the exposed beams of the ceilings, the interior of the log walls, and the first floor beaded board partitions. At about the same time the exterior of the log walls was covered with clapboards, accounting for the present excellent condition of the squared timbers. All these improvements, since they disguised the early condition and character of the building, were removed during the restoration process.

Kieffer's two-story log house lay in the path of the Genesee Expressway during that highway's construction. The New York State Department of Transportation, recognizing the structure's rarity, made it available to the Museum.

Martin Kieffer's circa 1814 two-story log house was located near Honeoye Creek in the Town of Rush, Monroe County.

ROADS AND TURNPIKES

"Historians have ever considered the existence of roads as a line of demarkation between the civilized and the savage state of society," wrote Ulysses Hedrick in his *History of Agriculture in the State of New York.* The first wave of pioneers who struggled into the Genesee Country from the east needed no other reminder that they had entered a "savage state of society" than their dark surroundings of trackless wilderness inhabited by wild beasts and "infested" (the recurring term in early accounts) with rattlesnakes.

Wherever this vanguard had come from there had been some kind of road. Here there were none. In 1792 at Canandaigua, Oliver Phelps sat among two small frame houses and a few log huts ready to sell land to those who could make their way there, over the Indian path from Geneva. More Indian trails led westward to the Genesee River, a twenty-six mile stretch along the whole length of which only four families had settled.

Conditions were better in the south. Settlers moving up over the Susquehanna route could follow the road far-sighted Captain Williamson had had hewn through the forests and hills of northern Pennsylvania and the southern tier of New York to Bath where the Captain held forth in a village of his own making. From Bath, Williamson's road continued north and west another forty miles. Leaving the Susquehanna watershed this amazing road surmounted a range of hills and descended into the Genesee River valley to reach the Captain's infant settlement at Williamsburg.

As the region became more built up, roads radiated in many directions from the northern terminus of Williamson's highway.

The State of New York showed concern for the "savage state" of its western regions when it began to appropriate money for 'internal improvements.' In 1794 the legislature authorized a road to be surveyed between Utica and the Genesee River; by the end of the century stagecoaches were plying the route. When the demand for more and better roads outstripped the state's resources, private capital was encouraged to invest in toll roads. By 1807, sixty-seven turnpike companies had been chartered to build roads covering some three thousand miles throughout the state.

Several connecting turnpikes—principally the Seneca, the Great Western and the Cayuga—linked Albany and Canandaigua. From Canandaigua the Ontario and Western Turnpike carried on to the Niagara Frontier, by way of Batavia, headquarters of the Holland Land Company. The completion of this turnpike in 1813 (following essentially the same course as New York State Route 5 which passes within a mile of the present Museum site) helped end the relative isolation of the northern Genesee Country.

An old milestone from a place, according to its inscription, 13 miles from LeRoy and 14 miles from Brockport. Now at Genesee Country Village.

Western New York in 1809 - showing early roads which in most cases followed the well-worn old Indian trails. The circled inset, taken from a 1792 survey map of the Phelps and Gorham Purchase, indicates no road connection between Geneva and the County Town (Canandaigua); and the 1809 map, strangely, fails to identify the village of Canandaigua, which by then was a well-developed county seat.

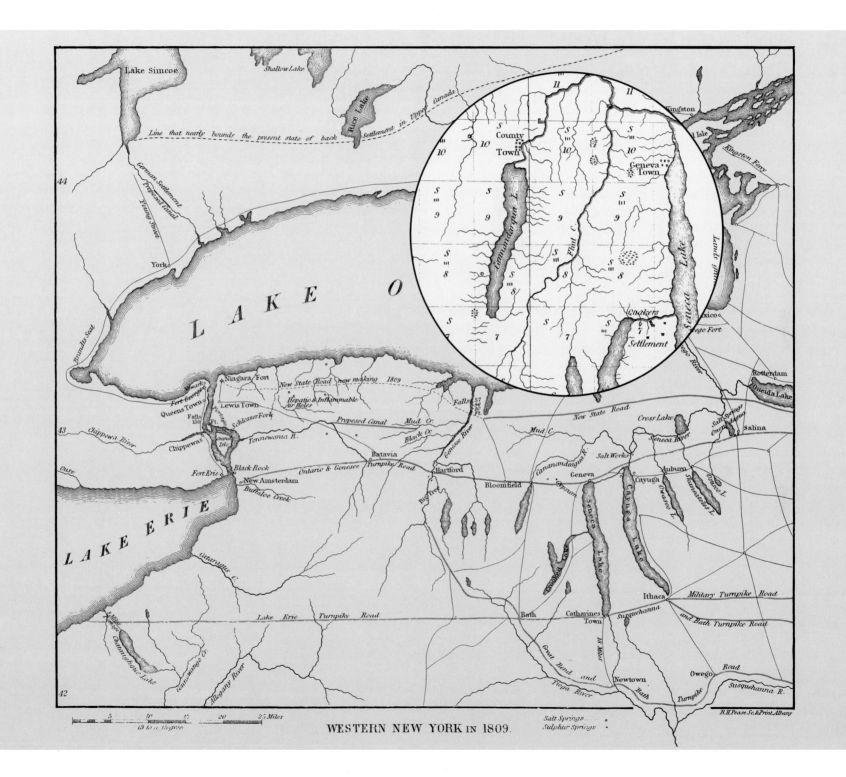

WESTERN NEW YORK IN 1809.

MORE ABOUT ROADS AND TURNPIKES

Over the "Genesee Pike" travelled tens of thousands of settlers, some staying to take up land in the Genesee Country, others going on to Ohio and Michigan. More important, agricultural produce could now reach the Albany market, bringing cash and a greater promise of prosperity to the Genesee farmer.

Eastward went hurrying and bouncing stagecoaches, slow droves of cattle, and heavy freight wagons laden with potash, charcoal, and wheat in two forms—grain by the bushel or whiskey by the barrel. Westward returned the four-in-hand stagecoaches, the drovers, and the wagons with mixed cargoes of hard goods for the trading posts, wet goods for the taverns, iron for the blacksmith, and supplies for the stores and shopkeepers.

In addition, "There was a pageant of foot travelers as well," according to Hedrick, "workmen, peddlers with their pack, the humble cobbler, travelers without money to ride, strange Indians, bands of gypsies, missionaries, strolling players, and all the odds and ends of New World humanity."

Turnpikes and sideroads alike were dirt, made as level as possible by removing stumps and stones, and by plowing, scraping and filling. In the rainy spring the roads were muddy and barely passable; in the hot summer they were dusty and heavy with sand; in the wet times of the fall rutted and muddy. The best season to travel was when there was enough snow to use sleds and sleighs. Large and sturdy bobsleds carried massive loads of freight over the frozen and snow-covered roads.

Maintenance of the toll roads was the responsibility of their proprietors. Originally public highways were constructed by the land companies to encourage settlement, agents for the companies offering settlers land in exchange for work on the roads. Later when the roads were taken over by the state they were maintained by laborers hired with road tax money or by farmers who preferred to work out their road tax with labor.

Within a few years would come the canals and within a few more the railroads, each greatly affecting the economy and movement within the Genesee Country. These new modes soon diminished the importance of roads as carriers of freight and passengers—but in the first quarter of the nineteenth century it was the highways and byways which moved the Genesee Country out of its "savage state."

The first plank road in western New York was a fourteen mile stretch near Syracuse in 1847-48.

The Rochester and Hemlock Lake Plank Road Company, organized in 1850, was one of many in the Genesee Country. The twenty-three mile roadway enabled teamsters to draw heavy loads of timber to the sawmills and lumber yards in Rochester.

The great advantage of plank roads was conspicuous when wet weather made other roads nearly impassable. But the plank surfaces did not hold up long under the heavy wear from the iron tires of wagon wheels, from the iron shoes of the horse and the decay from the weather and soon required repair and rebuilding. Excessive maintenance costs which exceeded the revenues from tolls forced the failure of the road companies. Most of the plank roads were abandoned by the end of the Civil War period. The tollhouse at the threshold of Genesee Country Village was the southernmost of the two Rochester and Hemlock Lake Plank Road Company tollhouses which flanked the village of Lima in Livingston County. The tollkeeper, his wife, three children and a boarder shared its two rooms, kitchen, and loft.

Rochester and Hemlock Lake Plank Road tollhouse, circa 1850, from Lima, New York.

THE TRADING POST

Because of the difficulty of transporting size-able loads, the settler brought along very few worldly goods as he ventured into the Genesee Country. Among the essentials he managed to include were his axe, his gun, a potash kettle, blankets, cooking utensils, salt, meat, grain seed, and bags of flour. He had been assured that his other wants could be filled at stores in Canandaigua, the northern point of entry, or at Bath or Williamsburg in the south. Unless he chose to settle within easy distance of one of these centers, the pioneer's trips to the store for supplies or mail would be inconvenient and time consuming. As settlement advanced there was a demand for stores or "trading posts" (to use a more descriptive and perhaps more accurate term) in the interior. The construction of roads made it possible for wagons to supply trading posts in the remote regions. The imported goods of the typical frontier store or trading post would include such commodities as tea and coffee; molasses, brown sugar, and rum; iron tools and nails; animal traps and gunpowder; pots and pans; baskets and buckets; flour and dyestuffs.

The pioneer farmer on his part might offer animal pelts, potash, cheese, butter, maple sugar, wheat, dressed flax, fresh meat or something knitted or woven by the pioneer's wife—in exchange for selections from the storekeeper's merchandise. With cash remaining scarce throughout the early period of settlement, the friendly storekeeper extended credit so that the pioneer farmer would not want for his family or his incipient farmstead. Twice a year, perhaps, was often enough to settle accounts—when the pioneer's harvest or the sale of potash earned him some cash.

The frontier store served as a post office and message center for the outlying settlers and was a clearing house for news about the young nation or from within the neighborhood. Just as the frontier store or trading post was of aid to the hardy and struggling pioneer it was also of benefit to the bustling land agent. The store's presence furthered settlement in its general neighborhood and boosted land values—and was often the instrument for the birth of a hamlet.

Thomson's Store Room is well supplied with the staples of the pioneer—for sale or for barter.

In 1807 at President Thomas Jefferson's urging, Congress passed the Embargo Act which placed restrictions on trade with Great Britain. That year Joseph Thomson, from Peru, Massachusetts, erected a one-and-a-half story building along the well-traveled road to Braddock's Bay.

His partner, David Tuttle, remained in Peru minding another store and sending on supplies to Thomson who was busy setting up a trading post in their new building on the western New York frontier.

Food and refreshment were available to those journeying through the area or coming to Thomson's for supplies. Drovers passing to and from the Niagara region found lodging for the night in one of three upstairs bed chambers. A large arched ceiling Meeting Room or Ballroom on the second floor could accommodate additional sleeping bodies when the place was over-crowded.

A large brick oven in the basement baked bread for nearby settlers whose rude dwellings did not boast ovens.

The inventory in the storeroom is based upon old account books from a store and trading post operated during the same period by John Tryon on Irondequoit Bay. Thomson's old place, which served as a store and trading post, an inn, post office, meeting place and bakery, came from Warren Adams, whose family has held the property ever since acquiring it from Joseph Thomson's heirs in 1845.

Thomson's Trading Post, circa 1807, from Riga Center, New York.

28

TAVERNS AND INNS

As roads were constructed in western New York in the last decade of the nineteenth century, settlers' cabins appeared at frequent intervals along them. Travelers discovered many of these cabins were identified by their owners as "taverns." "Tavern" was the name used to signify "inn," but most of the roadside establishments in the earliest years of the Genesee Country were hardly deserving of either title. To his dismay the worn wayfarer often found that the typical tavern along his route offered no beds and very little breakfast—or supper. Many of those who by necessity were forced to take refuge at such places preferred to sleep in their clothes on the floor. The option was to share a bed with up to five strangers—inmates of the cabin or other 'guests'—and unrestricted numbers of fleas and bedbugs.

The Viscount de Chateaubriand described one of his overnights on the way to Niagara in 1790: "...I stood stupefied at the aspect of an immense bed constructed around a stake; each traveller took his place in this bed with his feet toward the stake...like the spokes of a wheel...I introduced myself into this machine..." But the Viscount did not remain the night within the wheel of sleepers. "...I threw myself out of the bed and, cursing the usages of first settlers, went asleep in my portmanteau under the light of the moon."

Among the epithets applied by other survivors of a stay at one of these early hostelries were "filthy," "disgusting," "appalling," "hideous," and "wretched." Happily the sorry lot of the first generation of taverns and tavernkeepers was soon succeeded by a new breed of caring innkeepers who set up proper inns. At later establishments, located within the growing villages or spaced several miles apart along the main roads, even fastidious European travellers found the accommodations reasonably respectable and the food and refreshment wholesome and appe-

tizing. If, at most of the best inns in the Genesee Country, the guests had to eat simultaneously with others at a common table, at least they would have fewer bedfellows at night. The inn, particularly if it served as a stage stop, was a center for gatherings—formal and informal—and became an integral part of the rural community.

The tavern keeper's daughter kibitzes a game of draughts.

In 1809 Sylvester Hosmer, one of five sons of Timothy Hosmer, physician, married Laura Smith, one of the six daughters of Major Isaac Smith, innkeeper. The Major's tavern was a log building alongside the Ontario and Genesee Turnpike a few miles west of the Genesee river crossing near Avon.

Following his father-in-law's death, Sylvester Hosmer became its proprietor. Accommodations and food were pronounced excellent by those who stopped at the log inn while travelling the main route through western New York.

Business was good; and in 1818 Hosmer replaced his log building with the two-story frame structure which now looks across the Genesee Country Village square.

There are seven fireplaces throughout the inn. The brick floored kitchen and storerooms are on the ground level. The first floor includes a taproom (reached through an entrance at the side), a public dining room, a ladies' dining room and a ladies' sitting room. On the second floor are the landlord's own quarters, four private sleeping rooms, and a combined meeting and ballroom.

The old inn was occupied as a residence in its late years, although it was being used as a granary when acquired by the Museum. The inn-yard behind Hosmer's contains a wagon shed and Hosmer's old brick-lined ice house given to the Museum by Silvanus Macy.

Hosmer's Inn, circa 1818 - a holdover of the Georgian architectural tradition.

THE GENESEE FARMER

That better times for the Genesee farmer arrived sooner east of the Genesee River than to its west is suggested by the generally earlier appearance there of the "frame" farmhouse—a sure sign of prosperity.

Even though the sale of their lands had been disappointingly slow for Oliver Phelps and his associates, by far the greatest concentration of first round settlers was within their Purchase. But pioneer Ezra Jones, who did not arrive from Connecticut until about 1805, was still able to pick up 120 acres of excellent land for wheat in what is now Ontario County. There, in the midst of a settled area, he enjoyed the improved roads which placed him effectively nearer to markets at Phelps' Canandaigua and at Captain Williamson's Geneva.

The history of the Jones farmstead may be cited as a variation on the theme of the 'Pioneer's Progress' sketched by Orsamus Turner. The first dwelling of ex-Continental Army soldier Jones was of logs. It may be reasonably assumed that his next major plant improvement was a frame barn, although no trace of such a structure survives. On a 120-acre farm a proper barn would have had priority over even the unpretentious story-and-a-half frame house erected on the place in the 1820s. And this simple serviceable dwelling, with its summer kitchen wing dating from the 1830s, was demoted to the role of tenant house when a large two-story Victorian country house was erected in the 1860s.

Under such a succession of roofs (and owners) the old Jones farmstead reflected half a century of change in farmhouse architecture, accompanied most certainly by technological progress in the farmyard and fields and in the furnishings of the farmhouse itself. Archaeology undertaken at the site yielded hundreds of earthenware and metal remains which assisted the curators in keeping up with the Joneses when refurnishing the old farmhouse.

Considered alongside inventories of similar households, the siftings from the earth indicate that most farm families in the region had plain but good things.

About the farm itself—its fields and pastures, gardens and orchards, barns and stables—the tale is told through old diaries and daybooks and through contemporary publications devoted to agricultural matters. Of the many journals directed to the New York State farmer the one most immediate to this region was *The Genesee Farmer*. First published in Rochester in 1831 by Luther Tucker, it continued for thirty years.

The Jones farmhouse comes from Tileyard Road, near Orleans, in Ontario County. Its design, derived from Connecticut precedents, is typical of the small early nineteenth-century Genesee Country timber-framed and clapboard-covered farmhouse.

During the early part of the nineteenth century itinerant artists worked their way through the Genesee region, their trail marked by the stencilled walls of houses in the villages and in the country. The work of individuals among them can sometimes be traced through their repeated use of favorite motifs.

Undoubtedly some of the stencilling was homemade — done by the owners themselves or a clever friend. Whoever executed the stencils in a bed chamber of the Jones farmhouse never troubled to move the furniture. Gaps in the design clearly indicate the location of the bed, a blanket chest, and a bureau.

The Ezra Jones Farmhouse from Ontario County, New York, circa 1820 (with circa 1830 summer kitchen addition) was given to the Museum by the Gillam brothers.

On the walls of the Jones parlor the faded work of the original stencil artist contrasts with the fresh colors of reproductions where replastering of damaged walls was necessary.

THE VILLAGES

The land companies and their agents never doubted that where the Iroquois formerly hunted and fished there would one day be towns and cities. Commerce, they reasoned, would inevitably follow the conversion of forests into productive and prosperous farmlands. The speculators looked upon locations alongside navigable waterways and their overland connections as the most likely place for concentrated settlement.

Captain Charles Williamson, agent for the Pulteney interests, was guided by some such thinking when he selected the sites of Bath, Williamsburg, Sodus, Lyons and Geneva. Oliver Phelps, the first land agent in the Genesee Country, also made a wise choice of site when he laid out Canandaigua and established his headquarters there. The construction of the Ontario and Genesee Turnpike confirmed Canandaigua as the northern point of entry to the Genesee Country and insured its steady progress for a quarter of a century.

On the other hand, few of the "centers" (with land set aside in each for future churches and schools) which Phelps' surveyors drew up in his townships ever fulfilled the agent's expectations. Many were bypassed when geographic considerations determined where roads could be built most expeditiously.

Villages were more apt to come about through economic opportunities at bridgeheads and water-falls or where main roads intersected. More than a dozen still thriving communities along the seventy-five mile stretch of New York State Route 5 owe their birth and longevity to their position where north-south roads or streams met the old Ontario and Genesee Turnpike.

The alert innkeeper or storekeeper might be the first to see the chances for a livelihood and profits by locating at a busy junction. An enterprising black-smith might set up his forge nearby, soon followed by the wheelwright and wagonmaker. Then would come the housewright, the joiner, the cabinetmaker, and perhaps the maker of boots and shoes. Any special advantages the location offered, such as a stream for the tanner, a head of water for the miller, clay for the potter and brickmaker, a quarry for the builder would, of course, add new dimensions to the character of the settlement. As the hamlet swelled, other tradesmen would set up shop, and the doctor and the lawyer would deem the growing community a suitable place to establish practices. Further development would justify the organization of an incorporated village and the election of officials.

Within a decade a favorably-situated Genesee Country rural village could become a shipping point and marketplace for the farmer, a bustling hub for other country commerce, a stopover for the itinerant artisan, and a place where an honest man might find work. Still, hundreds of western New York hamlets remained small, quickly reaching the point destiny intended for them. Expansion was possible only through the happy combination of a number of favorable conditions: reliable transportation to the large markets; convenient sources of energy and raw materials; a ready supply of labor, leadership, politics and luck.

"The Young Lion of the West," as Rochester liked to regard itself in its boom days, drew off skilled workers, seasoned professionals, experienced leaders, capital, imagination and opportunity from all sections of the Genesee watershed. At the same time the great gristmills of the "Flour City," together with the Erie Canal, were agents for the remarkable prosperity of the Genesee farmer in the second quarter of the nineteenth century—a reward reaped in part thanks to the paths and fields cleared by the pioneer in the first quarter.

"Bird's-eye views" of villages, towns, and cities were produced throughout most of the nineteenth century but enjoyed their greatest vogue during the last quarter of the century. This rare view of West Bloomfield, New York, represents its appearance in the glory days of the Ontario and Genesee Turnpike.

THE EARLIEST HOUSE IN THE VILLAGE

Amherst Humphrey's c. 1797 house, though of a type common for well over a century in his native Massachusetts, was ahead of its time in the Genesee Country. His ten-room "framed" house would remain conspicuous among the log houses of other pioneers then settling in the area.

The route along which Amherst Humphrey settled had only five years earlier been an Indian trail between Canandaigua and the Genesee River with less than a handful of families residing within the twenty-six mile stretch. Work was yet to begin on the Ontario and Genesee Turnpike which one day would carry its heavy traffic within yards of his front door.

Little is known about Amherst Humphrey, but some assumptions may be hazarded from the meager facts at hand. He was a farmer. Where today there is corn on his old farmlands, Humphrey undoubtedly raised wheat. He was elected Pathmaster of his road district in 1798 and in 1806 he became Overseer of Highways for the district. It seems historically logical to believe that he would have been closely involved with the construction of the vitally important turnpike through his district and right past his farm.

More is known about the house of Amherst Humphrey than about the man himself. Houses like Humphrey's, organized around a central chimney system, were basic and logical. There were no hallways—the rooms interconnected. A large fireplace was a necessity for cooking and an oven was needed alongside it for baking. An iron crane swung from one side of the fire chamber, supporting the kettle; on the wide hearth was room for food needing heat for its preparation or warming for its serving.

Two other fireplaces heated the two front rooms. These were smaller, nestled back into the mass of masonry needed to contain the kitchen fireplace and oven, and used the same central flue.

The central chimney accommodated a fireplace on the second floor as well, furnishing welcome heat to the largest of Humphrey's five second-floor chambers.

The great pile of masonry in the central chimney type house served as a solid anchor for the structure's heavy timber frame, portions of which might rest against the chimney. While Humphrey's fireplaces, oven, and chimney are of brick, the base beneath in the full cellar is of stone and contains its own fireplace opening—probably used for the messier business of lye-making and lard rendering. The floor of the basement is of cobblestone. There is a cistern beneath the summer kitchen (added in the 1830s) and an inside privy at the far end of the attached woodshed.

The decision to acquire Amherst Humphrey's farmhouse for a place on the Genesee Country Village square was made only after careful consideration of several houses of the same type in actual village settings within the local region. There was little to distinguish this country version from its town counterparts except for the view from its windows.

The Amherst Humphrey House, like thousands of story-and-a-half New England precedents from which it derives, is almost totally lacking in exterior ornamentation.

Yet the interior features include not only panelled and moulded doors, door and window surrounds and chair rails, but also mantelpieces and cupboards carried out in mouldings hand-planed by a craftsman with a light touch and an eye for proportion. Remarkably, the work of the unknown craftsman survived a century and three quarters of continuous occupation as a working farmhouse. Humphrey and his wife had raised four boys and five girls. Presumably the sons helped their father with the wheat and with the farm chores. The daughters could hardly have been idle. It is safe to assume they helped their mother with her work when they weren't attending a one-room school.

And it is tempting to imagine they may have spent some time at the treadle loom — as a costumed woman in the Village does each day in the Humphreys' old summer kitchen. Many households included a loom, set up wherever there was space, with work in progress upon it — waiting for hands and feet freed from more urgent tasks.

The first floor bed chamber includes an eighteenth century chest-on-chest brought to Clarendon, New York by one of that place's earliest settlers. The parlor contains a corner cupboard which was found resting upon its side and serving as a grain bin in a dilapidated house down the road a bit from Humphrey's.

The Amherst Humphrey House, c. 1797, Lima, New York.

A NEW DIRECTION

In the late eighteenth century a number of Scots settled near the "Big Springs" at the site of present day Caledonia. An important meeting place of the Indians, the Big Springs lay along the great war path of the Iroquois between the Finger Lakes and the Niagara Frontier. (The Ontario and Genesee Turnpike would follow the same trail.)

The Scots had been forced from their small farms in Perthshire by sheep-raising English landowners. Arriving in America, the Highlanders stayed briefly in the Mohawk Valley before being encouraged by Scotland-born Captain Charles Williamson to establish farms on the fertile land near the Big Springs.

Unlike his farmer compatriots who had set about raising wheat, John McKay, a Scot from Shamokin, Pennsylvania, arrived at the Big Springs as an entrepreneur. McKay had learned the ways of business from the redoubtable Captain Williamson, for whom he had worked first as a carpenter and then as superintendent.

McKay purchased Williamson's gristmill in Caledonia. Soon the canny Scot had acquired two hundred acres around the Big Springs and a mill site downstream at Mumford where he established a sawmill. McKay's mills thrived, serving settlers throughout a wide area within the Phelps and Gorham and the Holland Purchases. Another sawmill and a malt house at the Big Springs expanded McKay's operations. He shipped flour to Upper Canada and New York City.

By 1814 John McKay had prospered sufficiently to build the two-story brick-lined house which now looks out acrosss the Genesee Country Village square. The design of McKay's new house was as up-to-date as his ledger books. In the eastern coastal cities architects and builders were following the example of the Adams Brothers in England in refining the classical elements of the Georgian style. The American version of the modified style is termed "Federal" or "Post Colonial." Its lightened and attenuated forms are seen in the architectural detailing of the McKay house with its gable end turned toward the road. The elegant three-bay facade is articulated by four pilasters—linked by blind eliptical arches—and crowned by a full pediment.

Positioning the short side of a house to serve as its front had an important effect upon its interior plan: the narrow end allowed for only a single room across the front, with the entrance moving to one side. (The arrangement would become familiar in many Greek Revival dwellings.)

Much of the millwork and some of the furniture for John McKay's house was fashioned by Chester and Horace Harding, cabinetmakers and chairmakers in Caledonia, who later became accomplished portrait artists. Among the billings to McKay were: "Priming sash, $1.00; two bedsteads, $9.33; set of tables, $25.00; 13 chairs, $31.00; secretary (tiger maple), $45.00."

John McKay's fine house was to have had a full-height portico across its front; but when the four columns ordered for the job could not be shipped from Kingston, Ontario, during the War of 1812, McKay finished off his house without the projected frontispiece.

Some of the rear sections of this ample house were torn away in the early twentieth century. An archeological program conducted in cooperation with the Rochester Museum and Science Center uncovered the remains of the foundations of the missing portions, including footings for the kitchen hearth, fireplace and oven. In addition, the dig yielded hundreds of artifacts from the earliest period of occupation, providing useful information to guide the curators in equipping the house.

John McKay's old house and several pieces of his furniture were given to the Museum by his descendants, Mrs. Marianna Wilkins, Mrs. Mary Enderton and John Newton McKay.

McKay was a colorful character according to all accounts, including his own reminiscences. Friendly to the Indians who remained in the area in his day, he is said to have entertained Red Jacket and other Seneca chieftains. John McKay, like Sylvester Hosmer, took one of Major Isaac Smith's daughters as a bride.

One of McKay's reminiscences concerned someone else's bride. "I have often heard of buying wives," he wrote, "but have known, I think, of but one actual sale, and afterwards peaceable and quiet possession. Phelps, the early settler at Queenston, was a Ranger. In 1794 or '5, getting tired of a bachelor's life, he went to Geneva, bought the wife of one Jennings, for six hundred dollars, cash down, taking her directly to Queenston. I have heard that the transfer was a fortunate one for all concerned; she making him a good wife."

A c. 1985 sleigh ride party passes in front of the c. 1814 John McKay House.

AN OLD DIRECTION

Practical considerations guided Duncan J. MacArthur, another Scotsman, who in 1833, brought his bootmaking trade, his wife, and a one-year-old son to the Genesee Country. His house was small and in a form which looked back to one of the earliest houses of New England—the "salt box."

The first houses in the English colonies were one-story single-room affairs with a chimney at one end. Then came the two-room version with the chimney in the middle. Space could be added to either of these simple, gable-roofed boxes by adding a shed, or lean-to at the rear. The shed roof of the addition might carry out the same pitch as the main roof or it might be somewhat flatter. Whichever the case, the result was a long roof at the back and a short one in front, forming the "salt-box" shape.

Early salt-boxes grew from necessity; but their practical form for cold climates—with the longer roof slope to the north—has proven pleasing enough for the style to endure to the present time.

MacArthur's salt-box, built at a country cross-roads west of York Center, New York, evolved from a story-and-a-half house to which at some unknown time a lean-to was attached. The lean-to, which contains the kitchen, a borning room, and the pantry, is connected to the older portion of the house through the stair hall leading to the front entrance and through a door into the parlor. On the second floor is a single bed chamber.

For some twenty years in his cozy salt-box Duncan MacArthur ate, slept, and made good boots and shoes and a good living for himself, his wife Elizabeth, two sons, and a daughter. He not only made shoes for his children, but taught his sons how to make their own. In 1855 the prospering boot-maker moved into York Center where with his shoemaking sons he maintained a shoe store in a handsome two-story cobblestone building at the main four corners of the village.

The parlor of the 1831 Duncan MacArthur House is provided with simple cottage furnishings of the period and a striped hand-woven wool carpet.

Two important old features turned up during restoration work on Duncan MacArthur's old place. In the pantry a wooden sink, its drain intact and protruding through an outside wall, had been concealed when a twentieth-century addition was attached to the sunny side of the salt-box. At some earlier date the fireplaces in the kitchen and the parlor were both removed, their functions taken over by stoves. While the parlor mantelpiece was discarded, the kitchen mantelpiece was retained as a shelf on the rear wall. The narrowness of the chimney structure as indicated by the floor framing precluded the location of an oven in its usual position alongside the fireplace. But the chimney's depth left room for an oven with its opening on the side—a rare solution, dictated by the limited space of a small kitchen.

Colloquially, Duncan MacArthur's salt-box was called a "half house," a term which suggests that a "whole" house could be built by adding a structure with two windows on the other side of the front door, the rosy hope of the man who could afford only the "half house." In York Center there are examples of "whole" houses of the same vintage and with the same tall proportions of doorway and windows as MacArthur's, lending plausibility to the notion that the shoemaker's house was only a fraction of what it could be. Like half a pair of shoes.

Fronting the c. 1833 MacArthur House, the round picket fence came from an old homestead on Ridge Road in northern Monroe County.

TOWARD A NEW STYLE

The Holland Land Company's four million acres, which lay almost entirely west of the Genesee, were not offered for sale until ten years after settlement was well underway in the Phelps-Gorham Purchase east of the river. Yet in 1818 Joseph Ellicott, the Holland Land Company's agent, reported that the best farm sites had been sold.

However, at the same time, Ellicott and his company were troubled by an increasing number of defaults and departures. Large numbers of settlers, not satisfied perhaps with second best land they had agreed to buy, had packed off to Ohio where land was cheaper and just as arable. These desertions left the company with no payment received and some partially improved lands to dispose of. The agent, by offering the land on liberal terms, welcomed any new settlers who would help pick up the pieces.

Such was the situation in 1826 when Charles Foster brought his wife, four sons and four daughters to the Genesee Country in a horse-drawn vehicle. According to family tradition two of the children rode in the potash kettle. The kettle would indicate that Foster expected to be clearing land. That the 58 acres he eventually purchased were on a hill would suggest that a better site was unavailable or beyond his means.

Foster's first house was of logs. When in 1836 he was able to put up a frame house the result was surprisingly sophisticated, without any known local precedent. His one-and-a-half story house carries post-Colonial (Federal) detailing on the exterior while the widely overhanging roof and the interior trim point to the newer Greek Revival style. Such a combination of modes is often the result of an owner's reluctance to cast off all familiar forms and his tentative acceptance of the new.

The entrance of the Foster-Tufts house is of special interest. Fluted pilasters extend to the frieze, enframing not only the front doorway but the window above. These two elements are separated by a projecting shelf with egg and dart moulding.

Inside, a bridge-like landing above the entrance hall and behind the window receives the delicately detailed stairway and provides access to the upper bedrooms on both sides of the house. This landing, floating free from the front wall, permits light from the window above the door to reach the entrance hall below. An unusual feature is a tiny bed alcove set off from the dining room by an arched opening. One of the Foster daughters married Ely Tufts; ultimately three generations of Tufts occupied the house before it was turned over to secondary usages.

The house was in precarious shape when acquired by the Museum. It had served as a chickenhouse for some time and had lost its kitchen and woodshed wing to the elements. In its restored state it appears very much as it did when new in 1836. The furnishings include late Federal and early Empire examples.

Foster-Tufts House, c. 1836, Genesee County, New York.

The Foster-Tufts parlor with its painted floor cloth. A 'slipper room' (small bed chamber) off the parlor was for the use of an elderly resident.

Three styles of domestic architecture on the north edge of the Village Square.

THE ARRIVAL OF A REVIVAL

In Genesee Country Village over a dozen buildings dating from the 1840s and the 1850s are identified as variations of the Greek Revival style, their white-painted and diverse forms conspicuous on the village landscape.

Many arguments are put forth as to why the fashion for the Greek came about when it did — in the second quarter of the nineteenth century. There are both ideological reasons and practical.

In many instances the Greek style was accepted as symbolic, although the meaning of the symbol varied. For the nationalistic citizen of the still young Republic, which had twice waged war against the British, the new look was a continuation of the American resistance against things English. English designers had influenced the American Federal style at its outset; but now, it was felt, English architects had over-refined and enfeebled the product. The simple dignity of the classic Greek was needed to restore architectonic strength to the idiom.

The citizens of the republic claimed the Greek Revival as a purely American translation of ancient Greek architecture. It was true — the Grecian style was much more widely adopted in the States than in England. The conservative mind saw the restrained elegance of the Greek model as a check against the capricious "Gothic" which had begun to raise its pointed head.

For the liberal thinking Jacksonians the use of Greek patterns was a reminder of the democratic ideals of the people of ancient Greece and a tangible indication of American sympathy for the Greek struggle for independence from the Turks (1821-1832).

The practical side was more persuasive to architects and carpenters. The architects found the Greek massing and bold detail appropriate for the monumental buildings they were being called upon to design. The architectural handbooks of Asher Benjamin, Minard Lafever, and Edward Shaw enabled country carpenters, working with a "saw in one hand and a book of instructions in the other," to provide their clients with houses and shops and churches in the latest fashion.

While the architectural handbooks gave a semblance of unity to the widespread dependence upon Greek models, different climatic and economic conditions resulted in regional variations. These differences also came about according to the degree of observance of the prescribed proportions and the amount of adherence to academic detail.

By the 1840s a Greek Revival vernacular, particularly in domestic architecture, had developed in central and western New York State which was quite distinguishable from the expression in eastern New York and New England as well as from the Pennsylvania versions. As Ernest Pickering noted in *The Houses of America*, "Here...(in the Finger Lakes district and central New York)...the triumph of the Greek Revival was complete."

A simple farm cottage built by Martin Ward in 1832 at Stone Church, New York, took on its Greek Revival trappings when it was enlarged and renovated in the 1840s. The veranda dates from the 1860s.

George Eastman (1854-1932), founder of Eastman Kodak Company, spent his early youth in and around this one-and-a-half story Greek Revival dwelling in Waterville, New York. Eastman's father, who had been a nurseryman in Waterville, moved the family to Rochester where he founded a business school. At the death of the elder Eastman young George and his mother lived for a time on Livingston Park (near the residence of Dr. Frederick Backus in the house now facing the Genesee Country Village square) where the widow Eastman took in boarders. George Eastman served as a clerk in a Rochester bank before turning to his pioneering efforts in photographic films and cameras.

None of the furnishings in the Eastman Birthplace were the Eastmans', but have been selected corresponding to the comfortable circumstances the family enjoyed in Waterville.

The main block of the George Eastman Birthplace is a clear and compact translation of the Greek temple idiom into the American vernacular. The essential elements of temple architecture — the post, the lintel, and the pediment — are here scaled down and rendered in wood. The broad porch is the podium of the temple; four fluted Doric columns carry the wide entablature (horizontal bands above the columns) which is capped with a fully developed pediment.

George Eastman Birthplace, circa 1840, from Waterville, New York.

A Big Old House Reborn

The completion of the Erie Canal in 1825 had a momentous effect upon the Genesee Country. It brought the pioneer era to an end. Governor DeWitt Clinton, who had long championed the canal, was the hero of the day. As he journeyed aboard the *Seneca Chief* from Buffalo to Albany he was met with joyous celebrations along the entire 363 mile route.

Along the canal established cities enjoyed accelerated growth—and new towns sprang up. Traffic on the new waterway multiplied. Horse-drawn packet boats carried passengers over its placid waters; mule-drawn barges moved freight at a fraction of the cost and time of overland transportation.

As the wheat from the Genesee farmers poured into Rochester's great merchant mills, barge loads of barreled flour headed for the eastern markets. The little town on the river enjoyed a boom unprecedented in the history of the nation. Visitors could hardly credit their senses as they witnessed the bustle and tumult of heaving and hauling and hammering and sawing. The brisk and highly profitable flour trade made wealthy men among the many millers, merchants, brokers, and shippers involved in the industry.

One of the entrepreneurs who fashioned a fortune from milling, banking, and speculative ventures in Rochester was James Livingston, a descendant of an old Hudson River family. In 1827 Livingston built one of the first grand mansions in Rochester's Third Ward, soon to be full of other columned monuments to their newly wealthy owners. In 1835 the house was sold to businessman Joseph Strong who three years later sold it for $10,000 to Dr. Frederick Backus, prominent figure in civic and cultural affairs, and an elected official when the City of Rochester was formed in 1834.

Backus made substantial structural alterations to the house, employing Greek Revival elements and detailing. A one-story ell attached to the main block permitted the doubling of the parlor, while the entrance hall and stairway were shifted from the front to the side. Stylish decorative alterations were made on the interior. These changes, some very subtle, record an important phase in the history of the structure and were retained in its restoration.

The interior decoration and furnishings have been selected to reflect the high style of the 1830s and '40s.

Following the Civil War, the house again underwent change. The kitchen wing was replaced by a large brick addition, as the building was converted into a fashionable girls' school. For three-quarters of a century Livingston Park Seminary attracted genteel young ladies from the eastern United States.

When this important structure was threatened with destruction in the 1950s, a prominent Rochester benefactor acquired it and had it carefully dismantled and stored until an appropriate location and use could be found. In 1970 the benefactor found a location that satisfied his requirements. He presented the house to the Genesee Country Museum and shared in the cost of its reconstruction.

The Livingston-Backus House, c. 1827-1838, from Rochester's old Third Ward.

THE MERCHANTS

Something of the same nostalgia and aura of romance inspired by an old inn also surrounds the old country store. Only upon his retirement could the storekeeper share such impressions.

Storekeeping in the country was hard business. It is not to be wondered at that many a country store consisted of a partnership. Someone always had to mind the store.

Hours were long; customers could be cantankerous; old timers sitting around the stove could be ungrateful and tedious, their banter tiresome. Suppliers in the city could be too sharp; shipments might not arrive on time; perishables could spoil; debtors could be elusive or evasive; and the mail could be late. Profits could rarely have been extraordinary, particularly when split two or three ways.

The residence of the country storekeeper never rivalled the mansion of the merchant prince or the wholesaler in the city. Storekeepers often lived right on the premises, in tight quarters above the store.

The goods and services offered during store hours were indispensable to the well-being of the rural community, central to its economy. But work behind the scene when the shutters were put up was just short of endless. The little cash that came in over the counter had to be counted and put away; accounts had to be gone over; the store's own bills had to be paid; and orders had to be prepared. Judging from the bundles of invoices, statements, and order records which lay stacked in the upper storeroom of the Altay Store when it was acquired, Roswell Sheperd, Josiah Jackson and Charles Clark, the founding partners, had a complicated tiger by the tail. In addition to the normal handling of hardware, footware, groceries, notions, tools, books, and clothing over the counter, the partners operated a gristmill and a sawmill and shipped butter and eggs and other fresh things from the country to Elmira and New York City.

The Altay Store stocked most of the same staples as the old frontier trading post and sold or, like the trading post, bartered them away. But operations like those of the partners in the little hamlet of Altay were many times more complex than those at the pioneer trading post.

The Altay Store has a history dating back to 1819. The building which now houses it was built about 1848 when new owners took over the business. The structure's deep frieze, heavy cornice, and pilasters declare its debt to the Greek Revival style.

The store, located in the tiny Finger Lakes hamlet of Altay, closed its doors in 1899 and for the next seventy years the building stood unused. When it was dismantled and moved to the Village in 1970, it had suffered from disuse and decay, but there had been only negligible change to the interior.

Its counters, shelves and cupboards, although empty, were still in place. They are now stocked with hundreds of items of general merchandise corresponding to the store's own records from the 1840s, '50s and '60s, which were found intact in the attic of the building.

A mother and daughter watch as the storekeeper grinds some coffee; the man in the white hat watches the man in the black hat make his move.

THE DOCTOR

From the earliest days there was work for the scarce physicians in the Genesee Country. What few there were went about setting fractured limbs, stitching up slashes and cuts, mending broken heads, assisting at difficult confinements, lancing boils and carbuncles, and doing what they could for various other complaints.

But there was little any doctor knew that could help those settlers stricken with "ague" and the raging high temperatures and chills of "Genesee fever". Early travellers through the country often reported the prevalence of settlers suffering from the deadly fever. Indeed, Genesee fever (not recognized at the time as a form of malaria) took an indiscriminate toll among the pioneers. It came to be correctly associated with low lying watery areas—but for the wrong reason. The fever was supposed to come from decaying vegetation in such locations; in fact, like other forms of malaria, it was carried by mosquitos.

Robert Morris suggested a remedy to Captain Williamson when the captain was laid low:

"Dear Sir

> ...I fear you do not take good care of yourself, you should avoid Morning and Evening Dews and sleep Warm, live well and drink good Madeira wine, surely if these things are properly attended to, the Ague will abandon you and I hope to hear soon that it is gone..."

THE LAWYER

As soon as settlement built up in the Genesee Country there was work for the lawyer. While many agreements were of the handshake variety, the clearing and conveyance of land titles required the service of a lawyer if there were any complicated issues involved. Lawyers were needed to draw wills, to execute deeds and mortgages, to sort out and help resolve cases of disputed ownership. The lawyer was often called upon to represent landlords, land agents, and mortgage holders in actions against a delinquent farmer-settler. As one historian noted, "Lawyers served a society which by its political nature was litigious."

When towns and villages were being organized the lawyer was needed to prepare the formal documents. Many country lawyers embarked upon political careers and were elected to the state Legislature or Assembly. Some went on to become Congressmen; some became judges; some grew rich.

After an apprenticeship as a clerk in an established lawyer's office, George Hastings came to Mt. Morris, New York, in 1829 and hung out his shingle. For thirty-six years he enjoyed a successful practice, in the course of which he distinguished himself as a political leader, congressman, and judge.

In the early years of a settlement there were no doctors. But as hamlets and villages grew the doctor became, after the minister, the most prominent personage in the community. As Ulysses Hedrick records, "...the doctor who practiced in the country had learned his profession as a physician's apprentice, his first duties being those of a menial servant—cleaning bottles, tending the bell, sweeping the office, or at best, he drove the doctor's horses in the daily round of visits...

"...after four or five years of such apprenticeship, he sought some doctorless community and hung out his shingle. Then began a country doctor's life of hardship. Day and night, summer and winter, he was at the beck and call of every sufferer for miles about. He dispensed calomel, bled for all sundry complaints, vaccinated, sat at death beds, and helped to bury his patients."

Hastings Law Office, c. 1850, from Mt. Morris, New York.

Physician's Office, c. 1840, from South Valley, New York.

THE PHARMACIST

The drug store as a separate enterprise made a surprisingly early appearance in the Genesee Country. In the outlying areas the only source of drugs would be the doctor, except for some herb concoctions or nostrums a wife or a midwife might stir up. The doctor for the most part prepared his drugs himself in his own office and carried a supply of them with him in his saddlebag.

But in the larger villages there was enough demand to attract the services and skills of a man versed, if not professionally trained, in the art of preparing medicines, remedies, and drugs. Many of the druggist's compounds were prepared with no other guidance than a *Pharmacopoeia,* a massive tome giving Latin names, ingredients required, quantities needed, methods of preparation, the condition to be remedied, and the hoped-for results—everything but how much to charge.

Early in the nineteenth century the village pharmacist was likely to find himself in competition with the village doctor, both of whom were accustomed to prescribing and selling medicines for their customers and patients. But by mid-century, pharmacology and medicine evolved into separate and more scientific professions.

Along with a wide assortment of remedies and medicines which the pharmacist measured and mixed in his shop, he carried an impressive array of patent medicines and he often handled painters' supplies, colors for oils, window glass and perfumery.

The druggist kept his supplies and secret substances in an elephantine apothecary chest whose drawers also contained examples of his finished products—from a mild sedative to a mixture strong enough to kill a horse.

The old mortar and pestle trade sign was found in a shed.

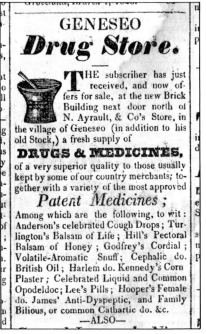

GENESEO Drug Store.

THE subscriber has just received, and now offers for sale, at the new Brick Building next door north of N. Ayrault, & Co's Store, in the village of Geneseo (in addition to his old Stock,) a fresh supply of **DRUGS & MEDICINES,** of a very superior quality to those usually kept by some of our country merchants; together with a variety of the most approved *Patent Medicines;* Among which are the following, to wit: Anderson's celebrated Cough Drops; Turlington's Balsam of Life; Hill's Pectoral Balsam of Honey; Godfrey's Cordial; Volatile-Aromatic Snuff; Cephalic do. British Oil; Harlem do. Kennedy's Corn Plaster; Celebrated Liquid and Common Opodeldoc; Lee's Pills; Hooper's Female do. James' Anti-Dyspeptic, and Family Bilious, or common Cathartic do. &c. —ALSO—

Advertisement from an 1826 Livingston Register lists many of the drugs and medicines of "very superior quality" carried in the village drug store.

For over a quarter of a century the building now housing the Drug Store stood empty close by the road in the Finger Lakes hamlet of Tyrone, a few miles from the Altay Store. (There were once two inns in tiny Tyrone, one of them a stage-coach stop. Like other hamlets which have been by-passed as travel routes are altered, Tyrone retains much of its nineteenth-century character.)

The building is representative of the Greek Revival temple form adapted to serve commercial purposes.

Drug Store, c. 1840, from Tyrone, New York.

THE BOOKSELLER

The presence of a bookstore in its midst was the mark of a settled community. Almost every farmhouse owned a Bible, either brought by the pioneer when he came or bought from a country peddler. But beyond the Bible and perhaps a few religious works, an almanac and a history, the farmhouse inventory included little printed matter. Though they were often too busy to devote much time to reading, the need to increase their knowledge was recognized by the farmers in the Town of Wheatland, who in 1805 established "The Farmer's Library." By 1830 the cooperative enterprise contained over fifteen hundred titles of standard reference works of history, biography, religion, geography, manuals of practical interest to the farmer, and a few novels.

A village bookseller carried about the same general line of reading materials, along with stationery and writing supplies, ledger and account books.

The bookbinder makes a cameo appearance at Genesee Country Village. His tools and equipment share space with the bookseller.

The Bookseller's shop, from Hart's Corners, Monroe County, is an early 19th century building which was recast in the 1840s with quaint and unconventional Greek Revival details.

THE PRINTER

A rural village was fortunate if there was a printer in its midst, particularly if the printer had the temerity and energy to print a newspaper. The printer was fortunate if he gained enough subscribers to support the paper. He was particularly lucky if at least some of his subscribers paid in cash.

The bargaining instinct was strong in country settings. Advertisers and subscribers alike were prone to bring the printer products of the garden or orchard or chicken or maple trees in exchange for notices of a cow for sale, of a horse that had strayed, a new arrival of merchandise at the store, or a new line of printed cottons at the draper's. A bushel of apples, perhaps, was good for a six month subscription to the weekly newspaper which carried advertisements on all four pages (including the front page), legislative reports, the proceedings of Congress, poetry, anecdotes, letters from abroad and months-old "news" and editorials reprinted from distant and foreign papers.

Whether it was putting together a newspaper or printing broadsides and handbills, the printer set the type and well-worn woodcuts by hand. He then locked the form with wooden quoins, placed it upon the bed, applied ink with a leather tampion, laid down a sheet of paper and pulled the big handle on the press. The printed sheet was hung to dry. Later it would be folded to produce a four-page rural weekly.

The printer's equipment consists of a mid-nineteenth century Washington-type press, several cases of old type faces and woodcuts, a proof press, and many other early items gathered from area print shops.

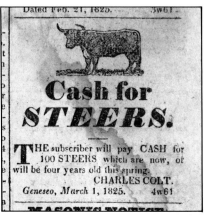

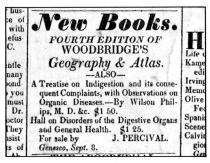

Excerpts from Genesee Country newspapers from the 1820s.

The two parts of the Print Shop were once separate shops along the main street of Caledonia, New York. They were moved in 1850 and joined to a larger house; there one served as the dining room and the other as the kitchen. The Greek Revival front portion dates from about 1835; the rear section is older, circa 1820.

THE BOOT AND SHOE MAN

As often as other members of his family went barefoot, the pioneer farmer himself, for the rough work of chopping and clearing away the forest and to keep his feet from freezing in winter, needed a pair of boots. He could hardly have set out for the Genesee Country without boots. His wife could make him a new shirt or pair of trousers when those items finally yielded to their daily abuse; but she could not replace her husband's boots when they gave way. The desperate pioneer or his valiant wife could manage some primitive restoration but to repair a leather boot properly required special tools and skills.

The cobbler and the bootmaker had the tools and the skills. Strictly speaking, the cobbler's specialty was repair; the bootmaker made the whole article. Each could perform the other's work, and in practice in the country both the distinction and the division of labor were ignored.

The itinerant cobbler or bootmaker, a familiar and welcome figure in the east, showed up in the Genesee Country whenever or wherever it was sufficiently settled to afford him steady work. Some itinerant bootmakers farmed in spring and summer and only travelled during the winter.

A village of sufficient size offered a livelihood for the journeyman bootmaker who would settle down and open a shop. The workshop of boot-and-shoemaker could be almost anywhere. It might be in a corner of his house.

The bootmaker's work required very little space, enough for his low bench and perhaps a table. He could make a pair of boots for about two dollars, a pair of men's shoes for a little less (although few men wore anything but knee-length boots). Even if he was kept busy making new boots and shoes and repairing old ones for his customers, the bootmaker would occasionally find time to make shoes for his children.

"THE OLDEST INSURANCE OFFICE IN THE UNITED STATES"

A faded photograph shows Delancy Stow in a filled out three-piece suit standing beside his black spaniel under the portico of his office building. Behind him, flanking the doorway and attached to the front wall, are several lithographed metal signs identifying the insurance companies represented by Stow and, before him, his father, William Stow.

The association between the Stows (both of whom practiced law) and the insurance business began when the elder Stow built the one-story office for his legal practice and insurance business in the canal town of Clyde, New York, in 1825—early enough for the Stows to call their little building "The Oldest Insurance Office in the United States", a claim subject to challenge, perhaps.

The Erie Canal had just been completed when William Stow set up his ventures. In addition to carrying on his legal practice he sold passage on the canal and insurance to canal shippers. Life insurance might come along later, but William Stow did well enough selling fire, accident, and marine insurance. After his son Delancy was admitted to the bar in 1862 the two worked as partners for nearly twenty years. When the elder Stow died in 1880, Delancy Stow carried on alone until his own death at age eighty-three in 1925—ending just a century of "business as usual" in "The Oldest Insurance Office in the United States."

About 1820 in East Avon, New York, a young lawyer built this small frame building and set up practice. According to local legend the lawyer left the village on horseback one day with an important sum of money. While the horse returned, the lawyer and the money were never seen again. A bootmaker later occupied the place.

The contrast between these two buildings, erected at approximately the same time to serve the lawyer's purposes is striking. The "Oldest Insurance Office", painted and porticoed, is adorned with delicate Federal architectural detail. It was a product of its place, a thriving canal town. Its drab neighbor's place was the yet to bloom crossroads hamlet of East Avon.

The Bootmaker's Shop, c. 1825, from East Avon, New York.

The Delancy Stow Law and Insurance Office, c. 1825, from Clyde, New York.

THE BLACKSMITH

He might have been preceded by the innkeeper and the storekeeper, but the blacksmith was the first tradesman to set up shop in the emerging village. He supplied goods and services basic to the welfare of any early community large or small. Even the tiniest hamlet included at least one blacksmith.

The smith shod horses, made hardware, repaired wagons and plows — everything of iron which the farmer or the villager could not repair himself. His trade was often combined with that of the wheelwright, with whom he might collaborate in making wagons and carriages.

Levi Rugg, whose shop is now in Genesee Country Village, was engaged in the two related occupations — smithing and wagon repair. His wagon shop was handy to the cobblestone blacksmith shop then owned by blacksmith William Bradley. Rugg's own smith was across the street from Bradley. This congestion of like and competing enterprises was common in the world of the blacksmith and illustrates some of the economics of the early nineteenth-century village. There may not have been a blacksmith shop on every corner. But in the average village there were more blacksmith shops than cobbler shops (which suggests the farmer's horse wore out his shoes faster than the farmer, perhaps because the horse wore twice as many).

Levi Rugg eventually bought the cobblestone shop, moved his operations into it, and ran a general blacksmithing business there until his death in 1875. Two succeeding smiths worked in the shop until well into the present century. In the ten years Rugg's old shop has been in operation at Genesee Country Museum there have been a dozen blacksmiths and half a dozen apprentices. They have made thousands of nails and hundreds of hinges and latches, but they have never shod a horse.

THE TINSMITH

Among the "workmen of the road" who made their peripatetic way about the Genesee Country were the candlemaker, the tailor, the weaver, and the cobbler. Another nomad appeared as soon as the condition of the roads permitted—the tin peddler, the original 'Yankee peddler.'

Doing very little tinsmithing himself — he was a peddler, not a craftsman. However, journeymen tinsmiths did set up shop in some Genesee Country villages.

The tinsmith retailed some of his shiny output; some was painted and decorated and wholesaled to the storekeeper. Now characterized as folk art, particularly fine and rare examples of "tole"—as painted tin is called—have brought as much at auction as an honest tinsmith might earn in a year, or a sharp Yankee peddler in six months.

The Tinsmith fashioning a punched tin lantern in the c. 1860 shop from Buckbee's Corners, New York.

Levi Rugg's Blacksmith Shop from Elba, New York, is representative of a nearly unique regional architectural expression—the cobblestone building. Beginning in the 1820s and until around the middle of the century, cobblestone structures were built in western and central New York State by the hundreds. They ranged from large public buildings to residences and small commercial structures.

The carefully selected stones came from two principal sources— the shores of Lake Ontario and the drumlins left by glacial retreat. Students of cobblestone architecture recognize distinct phases in the art— from the first simple coursing of medium-sized cobbles to the later patterned coursing of small and sometimes specially shaped cobblestones. The Rugg Blacksmith Shop, typical of the earlier phase, was built about 1830. The inside walls are rubble masonry.

The lengthy but vain search for an old tinsmith shop led to the substitution of an abandoned blacksmith's shop from Buckbee's Corners, a crossroads west of Rochester. It was at this same crossroads where Frank Mayer in his blacksmith's apron met the stagecoach bearing the woman who had crossed the Atlantic to become a blacksmith's bride.

Cobblestone Blacksmith Shop, c. 1830, from Elba, New York.

The Wagonmaker

Wagons would have been as useless to the first settlers as musket balls without muskets. There was plenty of game where they were going but there were no roads. If somehow the Yankee emigrants on the exodus from their stony hillsides of New England rode as far as Schenectady in wagons, they rode them no further.

From that jumping-off place they would travel either by water or over old Indian trails by packhorse. Most chose to load themselves and their goods into boats called "Schenectady bateaux," to be poled upstream on the Mohawk River, portaging around Little Falls. Navigation on the Mohawk ended near Fort Stanwix. The water route then continued via a series of portages linking Woods Creek, Oneida Lake, the Oswego and Seneca Rivers and finally the Canandaigua Lake outlet.

At Seneca Falls, the bateaux were emptied, the cargo being carried around them by Job Smith in his rudely constructed cart whose wheels were made from sawed off sections of a log.

Some of the emigrants left the Mohawk at Utica, preferring to make their way overland following paths worn through the forest by generations of Indians, rather than endure the wearisome portages. Emerging at Seneca Lake near Geneva, they pushed on to Canandaigua and their destinies in the wilderness of Genesee Country.

As more settlers arrived the old Iroquois trails were underbrushed and widened sufficiently to permit the passage of an ox-drawn cart or sledge. During the 1790s these primitive roads were gradually upgraded and new ones were surveyed and built.

In spite of improvements in the state and privately financed main highways the interior roads of the Genesee Country remained rudimentary. One Thomas Slayton was on his way to Canada over a secondary Genesee Country roadway when his wagon broke down. He looked around, saw no sign of a village but liked what he did see, chopped down an acre or two, built a cabin and stayed. He would get his wagon fixed when he could.

There was work for the wagonmaker in the Genesee Country. He was not far behind the blacksmith in setting up shop in the larger villages, often locating near the smith on whom he depended for iron tires for his wagon wheels and iron runners for the sleighs and bobsleds he made. The blacksmith might make minor wagon repairs but the skills of the wagonmaker/wheelwright were required to mend a broken wheel.

During the pioneer era in the Genesee Country the settler's initial demand was an ox cart, rather than a wagon. A two-wheeled cart was more maneuverable over and around stumps and boulders in newly cleared fields — only one pair of wheels to manage and protect. If the pioneer had not managed to bring such an indispensable vehicle with him the wagonmaker could make him one.

Then, in time, as his fortunes progressed the farmer could go to the wagonmaker for a four-wheeled wagon – to be horse-drawn to and from the fields and back and forth to the village.

The farm wagon was so constructed to permit the box to be lifted from its wheeled undercarriage and mounted upon a pair of bobsleds. Heavy loads could then be easily moved over frozen fields and roads during the winter.

The wheels of a farm wagon were of such a height to enable it to clear furrowed harvest-fields, the outcroppings of bumpy meadows, rough and rutted lanes, and gateways trodden deep in mud by cattle. But they should not be of too great a diameter lest the box be too high for pitching hay onto it or for loading sacks from it onto a man's shoulders.

Necessity fixed the lines between too high and too low. Necessity shaped the requirements for wheels, shafts, axles, carriages, boxes — everything. The American farm wagon at its evolutionary best was a useful and portable example of folk art — carrying in addition to the farmer and his cargo a distinctive beauty in which form followed function.

A wheelwright's vise holds the hub as the wagonmaker fits a felly (curved section of wooden rim) to a 12-spoke wheel.

The Carriage Museum

Here, retired from active duty, are half a hundred horse-drawn carriages and other vehicles which in the 19th and early 20th century logged thousands of miles over Genesee Country roads, village streets, and the pavements of Rochester. While many of them attest to European ancestry, most are as American as the model T Ford — the horseless carriage which contributed to their retirement.

The Genesee Country Museum's collection of horse-drawn vehicles, most of them on exhibition in the Carriage Museum, were acquired from a number of private collectors within the region. Some, for example those of the late Alvah G. Strong's wide assortment of sport driving vehicles, were in mint condition when presented to the Museum.

Others were expertly restored by a pair of veteran detail-conscious craftsmen who honed their special skills at the old Caley & Nash Carriage Works. These previously-owned vehicles were sanded, primed, painted, striped, re-upholstered, polished, and re-equipped with appropriate lamps and other accessories — in short, they were returned to low mileage or showroom condition.

The assemblage presents a broad picture of two- and four-wheeled vehicles including examples of basic horse-drawn conveyances which characterized the 19th century rural scene; a selection of turn-outs which might have been found in a gentleman's carriage house; utility vehicles; sporting rigs; veteran vehicles from the harness track; smart pleasure carts and wagons; a doctor's buggy; some examples of the village wagonmaker's craft; and elegant carriages and coaches, products of large carriage manufactories such as The Brewster Company of New York City and Rochester's famous James Cunningham Company.

King's *Handbook of the United States* (1891) described the Cunningham works as "the largest manufactory of exclusive fine vehicles in the country comprising landaus, broughams, coupes, victorias, Berlin coaches and others…The Cunningham vehicles are widely known, and distributed through their branch offices at New York, Chicago and St. Louis."

The types of luxurious carriages mentioned in the Cunningham reference are all on display, representing a number of manufacturers. The Carriage Museum is also a haven for a gallery of large sleighs, small cutters and an example of a wagon box mounted on bobsleds. Other horse-drawn vehicles may be seen at various points within the village. At this writing a Conestoga wagon rests in the Blacksmith Shop awaiting the attention of both the smith and the wagonmaker.

A team of four papier-maché horses are harnessed to a 19th century Victoria carriage once belonging to Franz-Joseph (1830-1916), Emperor of Austria and King of Hungary. Papier-maché mannequin horses were used by harness makers to display their wares.

Three turn of the century vehicles of the James Cunningham Company include at right rear a Park Drag, at center a Town Coach, and on the left a rear entry Family Omnibus.

THE POTTER

In the kitchen and pantries of the Village are scores of examples of the Genesee Country potter's art, both lead-glazed earthenware (also called "redware") and salt-glazed stoneware. These relics survived generations of everyday use for food preparation and storage in the nineteenth century before —in more recent years—drawing the notice of antique dealers, collectors, and museum curators.

The work of regional potters has also earned the attention of archaeologists. Historical research and excavations conducted by the Rochester Museum and Science Center have widened interest in and advanced the knowledge of the area's early potters.

Of the several sites excavated, the best documented are the Alvin Wilcox Pottery (c. 1825-1862) in Ontario County and the Morganville Pottery (c. 1829-1900) in Genesee County. The lead-glazed earthenware produced by these and other early nineteenth-century rural potters included crocks, jugs, jars, and bottles; plates, bowls, pitchers and porringers; milk pans and butter churns; candle and cake moulds; drain tiles and flower pots; chamber pots and spittoons.

The country potter worked hard. For his earthenware products he dug the clay from a nearby pit, ground it in a pug mill (sometimes horse-powered), turned the simple shapes on his wheel, applied the lead glaze, fired them in his kiln, and then sold them at the pottery or carried them to storekeepers who would pay the potter in cash or goods.

With the completion of the Erie Canal, stoneware factories producing the familiar light-colored and blue decorated wares were established in towns along the waterway. Clay could be brought in from Long Island and New Jersey and the stoneware products shipped out readily on the canal.

Stoneware was fired at higher temperatures which fused the clay so that it did not have to be glazed, although a salt glaze was commonly used.

The insides of stoneware vessels were coated with "Albany slip," a brownish-black clay wash, to provide a smooth finish. By mid-century competition from the stoneware factories forced most of the rural earthenware potteries to close down.

Salt glazed stoneware and lead glazed earthenware in the Parsonage kitchen.

Fortunatus Gleason, Jr. and his son, Charles, operated the Morganville Pottery in Stafford Township, Genesee County, until about the time of the Civil War. By then most of the rural earthenware potteries in the region had succumbed to competition from the larger stoneware producers. But the Morganville Pottery turned away from jugs and jars, concentrating on earthenware flower pots and drain tiles for which there was sufficient demand. Through a succession of family-related potters the Morganville operation survived into the present century. Some time after the pottery was closed down the structure was moved away and adapted into a dwelling. The site became a dumping ground.

In 1973 the Rochester Museum and Science Center and the Royal Ontario Museum jointly excavated the Morganville site. Their archaeologists uncovered the building's stone foundations as well as the floors of two kilns, one inside and one outside the pottery structure. Also found were quantities of earthenware fragments which have helped to identify and document surviving examples of Morganville pottery, previously only attributed to Morganville.

The report of the archaeologists and an early twentieth-century photograph of the old building formed the basis for the replica of the Morganville Pottery at the Genesee Country Museum. The wares produced in the Museum pottery follow closely documented examples of those turned out by the nineteenth-century rural potters of the Genesee Country.

The Flint Hill Pottery; a reproduction of the Morganville Pottery, c. 1829-1900, Genesee County.

THE COOPER

Containers have always been a necessity in any household. They were crucial to the settler. On the farm, baskets were handy for light, dry, and loose things; earthenware jugs and crocks were fine for liquids; iron kettles contained the simmering stews and soups, the heating milk, and the boiling ashes.

But wooden vessels of various forms, sizes, and capacities were required where nothing else would do — or do as well — in the country and in the town. Wooden buckets drew water from the well to the kitchen and barn. They were used to carry feed to the calves and milk back to the kitchen, to collect and carry sap from the maple trees. There were wooden wash tubs, butter churns and butter firkins. Without some or most of these wooden wares the farmer-settler and his wife were inconvenienced.

There were not quite as many demands for wooden containers around the house in the village but flour, sugar, and salt were kept in them, and every well had its wooden bucket.

The storekeeper received flour, fish, rum, molasses, and pork by the barrel. Barrels traveled in the other direction carrying apples, cider, and vinegar. The Altay Store shipped butter and eggs to Elmira and New York City in wooden barrels.

The maker and supplier of round wooden containers was the cooper. Some farmers did a little coopering during the winter, turning out barrels, tubs, and buckets. Others made only the staves which could be used for barter or, even better, sold for badly needed cash. Barrel staves were one of the most important exports from the Genesee Country to Canada in the early nineteenth century.

As the economy and trade of a settlement grew, there was work for the full time cooper. The 'tight' cooper made barrels for cider, vinegar, whiskey, beer, and meat. The 'slack' cooper, less expert, made barrels which did not need to be watertight for shipping flour, salt, maple sugar, apples, and other fruit.

The cooper "rived" (split) the staves from pine or oak blocks, beveled and jointed them to fit together, shaped the botton to fit the "chine" (groove left to receive the bottom) and banded the whole affair together with hoop poles of hickory or oak.

It was not easy. A twentieth century cooper who made tens of thousands of barrels for a Rochester brewery stated that it took several years for a journeyman cooper to be able to make a barrel tight enough to hold beer and strong enough to be bounced about by a powerful man.

Sometime around 1805 William Rumsey built this structure along the Ontario and Western Turnpike in what is now the Town of Stafford, New York. Rumsey was a surveyor for the Holland Land Company and until his death in 1820 was one of the most influential settlers in the area. His house was said to be the first frame building west of the Genesee River. It was specified by Rumsey's wife who refused to live in a house made of logs.

The unusually sturdy construction is of special interest, the hand hewn members being formed into trusses. Because of the unique character of the framework, portions have been left exposed. The building is presently used to exhibit the tools and equipment of the village cooper.

66

Cooper Shop, c. 1805, from Genesee County.

THE GUNSMITH

If the pioneer settler hit a moving target with his big smoothbore flint lock fowling piece, he was lucky. Birds had to be shot before they took to the wing. If—for mechanical reasons—the pioneer's gun couldn't hit anything at all it could be taken to William Antis who, in 1790, set up a gunsmith shop in Canandaigua. Antis could repair the gun or sell his customer a new one for eight or nine dollars. A second hand fowling piece could be had for two or three dollars.

In 1803 the Remington Arms Company developed a system to mass produce gun parts; by the 1820s, the firm began to supply those parts to gunsmiths like William Antis. The state of the art changed significantly as the gunsmith gained access to the technology of the day. Rifles were available, and the year 1835 saw the end of "flashes-in-the-pan" (misfires), as the rain-proof percussion system was developed.

In the second quarter of the nineteenth century sportsmen required more accurate guns for target practice. The gunsmiths who provided target weapons produced a more accurate product than those being used by the military. As western New York lands were cleared, sport hunting dropped off and well turned-out sportsmen went off to the Adirondacks or the Catskills for deer hunting. Well-heeled nimrods were ready to pay handsomely for custom-made sporting rifles, and New York State became a major center for custom gun supply.

One of the most important gunsmiths in the state at that time was William Billingshurst of Rochester, who, for forty years beginning in 1840, produced both fine guns and well-trained apprentices, craftsmen who went on to become gunsmiths in the smaller communities of the Genesee Country. William Roberts, for example, established himself in Dansville, where he produced excellent guns, along with some unpredictable models with three or four barrels.

In 1873 Winchester put the first successful repeating rifle on the market. This innovation, together with the financial panic of 1873 which depleted the bank accounts of many sportsmen, marked the beginning of the end for the bench gunsmith. Many who found their old craft obsolete became factory machinists.

The demise of the gunsmith was but one of the casualties among skilled craftsmen brought on by the surge of industrialism following the Civil War.

GUN·SMITH.

Since the gunsmith was the most skilled tradesman in the community, his apprentice had a lot to learn. The master gunsmith was an accomplished woodworker and joiner. He could repair or replace gun stocks. He could forge metals and he knew how to heat-treat metals—both ferrous and non-ferrous. The skills and tools of the jeweler were required to make springs. To decorate patch boxes the gunsmith had to be a fairly competent engraver.

The gunsmith shop at the Genesee Country Village was moved in from Dalton in lower Livingston County where Jonathan Thompson, with his brother, Joseph, ran a general repair business when they were not busy farming. In the small shop Jonathan made and repaired guns when the occasion arose. The tools and equipment now in the shop came from the Amos Wood gunshop in North Hamden, New York. Wood apprenticed under A.D. Bishop of Decatur, New York. Examples of guns made by the two men are almost identical as may be seen in those displayed within the shop.

THE DRESSMAKER

The one-and-a-half story frame structure housing the Millinery and Dressmaking shop was built in Roseboom, New York about 1825. Like many small buildings in country villages, it was put to various uses over the years.

By the middle of the nineteenth century a ladies' hat trimming and/or dressmaking shop might be found in a small New York State town. It would be a means for a widow or otherwise single woman to eke out an existence. In addition to the wares she made to order, she did alterations, and she would supply small items for the home seamstress.

The shop was also her home, and she left only to go to the store, the post office, the station (for goods arriving by train), to church, to a customer's house in the village, or to her grave.

Dressmaker's Shop, c. 1825, from Roseboom, New York.

THE FLY TIER

Spring Creek has a brief run — from the Big Springs in nearby Caledonia north for just over a mile where it joins the Oatka Creek a short distance from the Genesee Country Museum. The creek may be short, but it has long been regarded as a premier trout stream. By the middle of the nineteenth century its fame among sportsmen led to the establishment of several fishing clubs along its banks. (One of these clubs is active today.)

At all seasons the creek's clear, cold waters flow steadily from the bountiful Big Springs, a source well known to the Indians and the origin of water-power for John McKay's gristmill. The Seth Green Hatchery, the first of its kind and named for the Genesee Country friend of fish and fishermen, is situated along Spring Creek, dependent upon its salubrious flow to fill its propagation tanks and ponds.

In 1828 the remarkable stream drew to its banks a man who would soon win the attention of sports fishermen. John McBride, newly arrived from Scotland, settled his family in Mumford. McBride excelled as a maker of lures for fly fishermen, and his dressed, or tied, flies found a ready market.

McBride was assisted by his daughter, Sarah, who went on to become as well known as her father for flies and better known for her scientific studies of aquatic insects. As a result of her observations Sarah McBride dressed her flies "after nature." She won acclaim for her articles published in national journals and for her flies, which won awards at an international exposition.

In the building marked by the gold-leafed fish trade sign, the simple tools and materials for deception used by the maker of flies have been assembled to demonstrate the art designed to fool the fish and delight the sportsman. In addition there are examples of rods, reels, and tackle which would have been found in the nineteenth-century tackle shop.

The former site of the building now occupied by the Tackle Shop has interesting historical associations. The one-acre plot is believed to be part of the land conveyed to Horatio Jones, a white captive of the Senecas, in reward for his services as an interpreter in the Indians' negotiations with the United States government. In Horatio Jones's day the plot was just a short distance from Williamsburg, the short-lived village founded by Captain Charles Williamson, and lay along the main route between the Susquehanna and Genesee Rivers.

The Fly Tier's Tackle Shop and Dwelling, c. 1840, from Livingston County. In the background is the cobblestone blacksmith shop.

Representational trade signs or devices, originally intended to "speak" to the illiterate, became decorative means to attract the eye at nineteenth-century shops and businesses.

THE BREWER

From the earliest days on the island of Manhattan, the Dutch brewed beer; and after them the English made both beer and ale. The first reference to a brewery in New York was Harman Rutgers' entry in 1711: "Today I brewed the first beer in my Brewery. May the Lord bless us in the work of our hand."

Beer was a welcome supplement to the Genesee Country pioneer's basic diet. The Indian made beer from corn but the pioneer preferred the cereal grain barley in his recipe. Beer could be brewed on the farm or in the home; but by the middle of the nineteenth century many villages in western New York State included a brewery, a distillery, or both.

Mumford and Caledonia — just a mile apart — each had a brewery in the 1830s. Alexander Simpson, owner and proprietor of the one in Caledonia, did a brisk business during the construction of the Genesee Valley Canal. He sent wagonloads of beer all along the route of the canal as far south as Olean, New York. In 1837, when the canal was completed, Simpson sold his business.

In 1794, Tench Coxe, a prominent Philadelphia economist and George Washington's Assistant Secretary of the Treasury, drew up a detailed plan for a new agricultural community which might be built in the unsettled regions of New York or Pennsylvania. He seems to have thought of everything. In addition to 804 houses — all of stone and brick but of varying values — Coxe's roster included 207 other buildings. Among them were a gristmill, four lumber yards, one church, two taverns, one malt house, one brewery, and ten distilleries!

When Lord Selkirk visited Geneva, New York, in 1803 he found that in that pleasant village Coxe's requirements for the ideal town had been exceeded — there were thirteen distilleries. (There was also the requisite one brewery.) The English

nobleman, who was traveling about observing industries in Canada and the United States, prepared drawings and descriptions of the Geneva brewery. His careful records were the basis for the design and organization of the reproduction early nineteenth-century brewery at Genesee Country Village.

The brewer checks the situation in the fermentation vats.

Portions of the old Enright Brewery in Rochester and an early timber frame structure near West Bloomfield, New York, were merged to form the present building. The big copper kettle on the third floor and all the wooden vessels and vats are arranged according to Lord Selkirk's account of "a modest facility for the manufacture of beer." The entire operation requires equipment on six different floor levels within the three-story structure.

The brewery structure appearing in the photograph burned in 1988 with all its contents. It has been completely rebuilt. The wooden vessels and vats were reproduced by a Finger Lakes winery cooper.

The Brewery; a reproduction based upon Lord Selkirk's description of an early nineteenth-century brewery in Geneva, New York. Hops Drying House is at right and the hops field is seen between the two buildings.

THE HOPS GROWER

'Hop tea' and poultices made with hops were among the pioneer wife's favorite home remedies. She probably started her hop vine with a cutting from a wild plant; two or three vines would have sufficed for her household needs. From the flowers of the vine—the hops—she made an infusion for adding to cornmeal bread dough. As Orsamus Turner noted in his description of an early farmhouse, "upon one side of the door, a hop vine, and upon the other a morning glory..."

But the real use of the hops flower was (and is) in the brewing of beer and ale. Hops added to the "wort" impart a mild bitterness which offsets the sweetness of the malt. Hops act as a preservative and impart a fine aroma. Good hops help make good beer—and good ale. Growing hops to supply the brewing industry assumed major importance in New York State shortly after 1800. By mid-century the state was the leading producer of hops in the nation. Although the greatest concentration of hops producers was in central New York in Madison, Otsego, Onondaga, and Chenango Counties, some hops were grown commercially in the northern parts of the Genesee Country.

Hops growing in the nineteenth century was labor intensive—from training the cuttings up poles and along the network of supporting strings or wires

to the baling in the hops press. But the harvest called for the greatest number of helping hands. When the industry was at its height in New York, pickers by the hundreds—mostly women and children—would come out from villages and farms to aid in the harvesting. For many it was a working vacation, enlivened with frolics and dancing in the evenings. Once harvested, the hops were taken as soon as possible to the drying house where they were spread out on a slatted, mesh-covered floor above a furnace or stove to dry. After being baled in the press, the flowers of the hops field were ready to be carted to the brewery to fulfill their time-honored role.

Hop harvest time in the mid-nineteenth century, from **Harper's Weekly**.

In western New York commercial hops growing was largely confined to Monroe County, which in 1879, with 9000 tons, ranked fifteenth in production among the counties. Although never of major importance in a region where so much land was given over to wheat and corn, hops production did help meet the demand of Rochester's many breweries.

John Flanigan, a farmer with four acres of hops in Greece, New York, erected this drying house some time shortly after the Civil War. Though unused for many years when it was acquired by the Museum, the twin brick furnaces, the drying racks and the storage room happily were intact. Also in one piece was a massive block of cut limestone serving as the threshold of the wide front door. When flipped over onto a skid for loading, the underside revealed four large expertly incised letters—"BANK." The institution from which the stone was withdrawn has yet to be identified. If the bank was a casualty of "the Panic of 1873" the date of John Flanigan's drying house would be somewhat later than now supposed.

Only one other hops house in Monroe County has been known to survive.

From an old **Harper's Weekly** comes this documentation of the steps in the hops drying process. The interior arrangement of John Flanigan's drying house is much like this nineteenth century magazine artist's version.

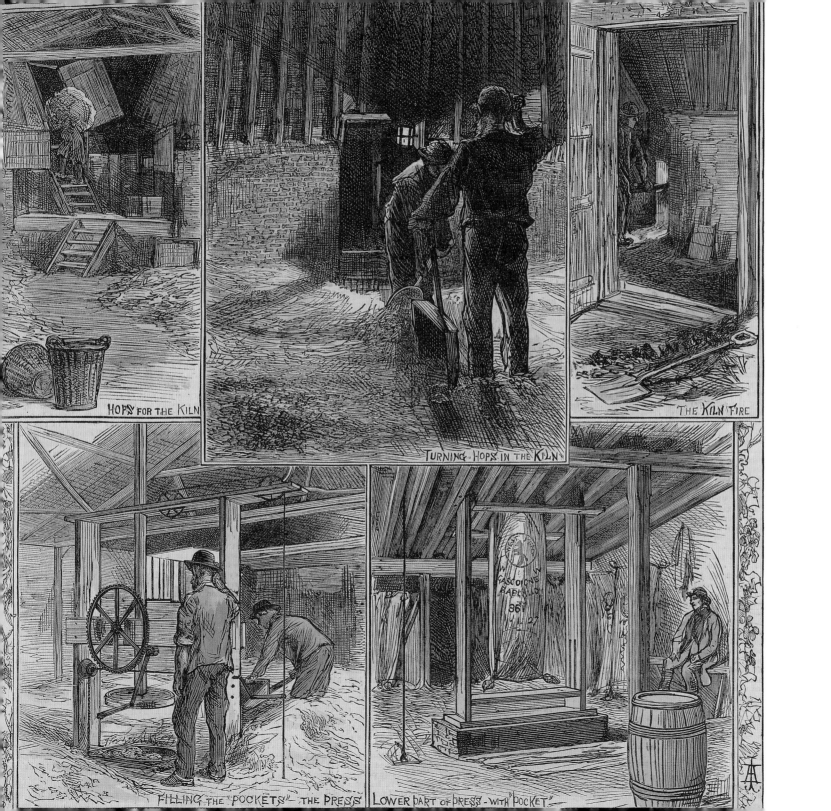

HOPS FOR THE KILN

TURNING THE HOPS IN THE KILN

THE KILN FIRE

FILLING THE "POCKETS" — THE PRESS

LOWER PART OF PRESS — WITH "POCKET"

Wool thread or yarn is spun on the large (sometimes called "walking") wheel, the spinner moving back and forth, turning the wheel with one hand while feeding the wool fibers to the spindle with the other.

To make linen thread the flax spinner sits at the wheel using both hands to separate and feed the long fibers of dressed flax to the reel - which is made to turn by means of the foot treadle.

On the loom dyed threads or yarns or rags are woven into materials with which to cover a floor, a bed, or a human being.

A quilt in process might remain on the frame for weeks or months, depending upon how much woman-power could be spared from other daily tasks.

Bread and pies are baking in the brick oven, a roast is underway in the tin oven on the hearth, and a stew is simmering away in a pot in the busy kitchen presided over by the hired cook in the Livingston-Backus House.

The cook in the Jones household is the mother; the clothes washer, ironer, and mender; the baby-sitter; the baker; the sausage stuffer; the butter and cheese maker; the housekeeper; and the farmer's wife. Here she has taken a bit of cheddar from the cheese safe to grate up for soup.

After the hard work of preparing her own splints from an ash or oak log, the basketmaker sits at her work using the principle of woof and warp and a nimble skill to weave a serviceable farm basket.

Some farmers grew small patches of broom corn for a cash crop and to provide raw materials for winter work on the farm, making a few brooms — another cash crop.

RELIGION

The settlers of the Genesee Country were citizens of the only nation in the world which did not have an official religion. What had been the state religion in the colonies under King George III—the Episcopal Church—was in disarray. Two-thirds of its clergy had fled the country at the outbreak of the Revolutionary War. The Methodist Church, too, had seen many of its ministers return to British jurisdiction. Many congregations were impoverished, and in the years following the war there was a falling away from the church as citizens busied themselves with building a new nation.

But the founding fathers had believed that there could be no national virtue without religious faith. In several of the original thirteen states discriminatory laws implied that since virtue depended upon religion then the state must support religion to make sure its people were virtuous. (New York was one of only three states where complete freedom of conscience existed.)

A series of religious revivals, beginning in Virginia in 1785 and spreading over the whole country, helped renew the nation's collective faith. Washington's farewell address reminded his country that "...reason and experience both forbid us to expect that national morality can prevail in exclusion of religious principles."

Genesee Country settlers came from communities where churches had been an integral part of life. Doubtless many pioneers had brought their bibles, observed the Sabbath, found time for private prayer, and felt the impulse to worship with others.

Contact with itinerant ministers—missionaries from several denominations—nurtured religious enthusiasm on the frontier and increased the shared desire of many settlers to institute regularly held church services. Congregations were formed and meetings were held in private homes. In 1790 religious services were held in a barn in Canandaigua.

In 1794 a minister from the Missionary Society of Connecticut preached to a large audience at Geneva, Big Tree, and Williamsburg. The following year a Presbyterian missionary organized churches in Lima and Geneseo.

The first meeting house in the Genesee Country, according to the reminiscences of James Sperry, an Ontario County settler, was erected in Bloomfield. "Two Missionaries from the East labored occasionally and sometimes continually in Bloomfield from 1797 to 1800. An extensive revival in that and adjoining towns continued under their labors for several years, and in 1801 they raised a large meeting house."

In 1844 Micah Brooks and his wife, Elizabeth, deeded to the trustees of the Methodist Society of Brooks Grove three-quarters of an acre of ground on which to build a church. They had originally purchased this land from Mary Jemison, "the White Woman of the Genesee." The Society's church rose that year, its strong Greek Revival lines topped off with a three-stage bell tower. In the recessed entrance a heavy entablature is supported by two Doric columns.

Inside, two enclosed stairways lead to the choir loft. The ceiling has a deep plaster frieze and cove cornice, and features a large plaster rosette from which hangs a three-tiered tin chandelier.

Brooks Grove Church was given to Genesee Country Museum by M.W. Brooks, great-grandson of Micah Brooks.

Brooks Grove Church, c. 1844, from Brooks Grove, New York.

The clean lines and soft colors of the sanctuary provide an atmosphere of quiet dignity. The old wooden-handled template for the plaster cove, discovered tucked away in the attic area, was used in the cove's restoration.

MISSIONARIES AND CAMP MEETINGS

But missionaries seemed reluctant to venture into lands west of the Genesee River. The settlers there, according to Lockwood Doty in his *History of Livingston County,* "paid little regard to the demands of the church, or indeed, to the mere ordinary restraints of order, and it was a common remark, current enough until the Scotch settlement was formed at Caledonia, that 'Sabbath day never crossed the Genesee River' ".

Then in 1805 Reverend Jedidiah Chapman, missionary of the Presbyterian Church, crossed the river and held Sunday services in Caledonia. "I preached in a large school house which was full and large numbers out of the door. The people are chiefly Highlanders from Scotland; they appeared not only decent and attentive, but very solemn. They expressed a desire, if I thought proper, to be organized as a Presbyterian church. I then appointed a conference for that purpose." The Scots soon put up a church building.

Meanwhile, a few miles further west of the river, three denominations were ministering to a less homogenous sprinkling of pioneers. In his memoirs Elihu Church recalled, "Our first religious meetings previous to the organization of the Congregational church, were held in my barn, it being the first framed barn in town. I think Elder Reed, a Baptist missionary, was the first to visit our settlement. The Reverend Mr. Phelps and several Methodist circuit riders visited us in the early years."

The revivals continued—including "The Great Revival" which began in Kentucky in 1801—bringing to church thousands of people. Some services went on for days with the inspired participants tenting out in what became "camp meetings." In 1810 DeWitt Clinton, while traveling the proposed route of the Erie Canal, attended a Methodist camp meeting where hundreds of people were listening to the heated discourse of forty-four ministers. Clinton and his companions were obliged to leave the campgrounds before the meeting was over. "...the voice of the preacher growing louder and louder reached our ears as we departed," his journal records, "and we met crowds of people going to the sermon. On the margin of the road we saw persons with cakes, beer, and other refreshments for sale."

While the fervor whipped up by the ongoing religious revival benefitted all Protestant churches, in the Genesee Country it was the circuit riding Methodist ministers who harvested the greatest number of souls. Their unpretentious dress and manners, combined with their vigorous preaching, made them popular in the rural areas and led to the formation of hundreds of Methodist congregations in western New York. By the middle of the nineteenth century, the Methodist Church enjoyed the largest membership of any denomination in the rural Genesee Country. The resulting church building boom punctuated the landscape with white painted Greek Revival houses of worship.

Where churches could so afford, housing was furnished the ministers to help offset the generally low salaries they received. The Brooks Grove Church, because of its importance in the regional Methodist Church affairs, provided a house to be used not only as a residence for its own minister but also as a place where the circuit leaders might hold meetings.

On the lot immediately south of Brooks Grove Church stood this one-and-a-half story frame house. It was built by Henry Jarvis in 1835 and thus antedates the church by several years. Although it was the church's long time closest neighbor, there is no record of its use as a parsonage until it was set down to serve that purpose at Genesee Country Village.

The parlor serves as the pastor's study and a place to receive visitors. All other activities of daily life in this small house are crowded about the kitchen. Like the Foster-Tufts house of similar date, the house that Jarvis built declares its architectural debt to the widening Greek Revival influence while retaining features, such as the fan light in the gable, associated with the earlier Federal style.

The Parsonage, c. 1835, from Brooks Grove, New York.

A RURAL ROMAN CATHOLIC CHURCH

By the 1820s several Protestant congregations had raised church buildings. As they vied for the souls of the settlers, the congregations also competed with one another architecturally. Bigger was better; stone or brick was superior to wood. Most country churches were wooden, but as congregations grew these first churches often were torn down and replaced with more ambitious structures.

By the 1820s immigration to western New York was no longer confined to the predominantly Protestant settlers from New England and the mid-Atlantic states. From Europe came German Catholics; and then in larger numbers Irish Catholics who found ready employment building canals. Some of these Irishmen turned to farming when the canals had been completed; others helped build railroads.

The first Catholics in the Genesee Country had no place to worship other than their own homes—an historical irony since it had been the French Catholic priests two centuries earlier who had built the first Christian chapels in the Genesee Country. (The French established four missions in Seneca territory and more than a dozen elsewhere in the land of the Iroquois.) As the Roman Catholic population grew, congregations were organized; and as early as 1823 a stone church, St. Patrick's, was raised by the Roman Catholic Religious Society in Rochesterville.

Toward mid-century, Catholic churches were built in some of the larger villages in the hinterland, and the country faithful could journey to a village to attend mass.

In Chili, a farming community west of Rochester, a group of Catholic families were for many years dependent for their spiritual needs upon masses conducted by a priest in their homes or by traveling to Rochester or Scottsville, several miles distant. In 1854 the men of these families set about building their own church. Within a year, with their own hands and without architect or contractor, they had completed St. Feehan's Church—and affixed a simple wooden cross at its peak. The cross remains there today at the church's new location at Genesee Country Village.

The land on which St. Feehan's originally stood was given by parishioner Patrick Golden who, it is believed, influenced the decision to call the new church after his family's old parish in the west of Ireland. Since the land where the good men of Chili built their church was low and inundated each year during spring thaws, St. Feehan's became known as the "Swamp Church." During the 1880s, the church was moved a short distance to the higher ground of Chestnut Ridge.

By the 1960s St. Feehan's ever-increasing congregation had outgrown its crowded quarters and moved into an entirely new plant which today has grown to a large circular church, a school, convent, and rectory. Reverend Donald J. Murphy made it possible for old St. Feehan's to undergo one more move—this time to a knoll above Thompson's Trading Post and Store.

The sanctuary of St. Feehan's had undergone many changes during its century of service in Chili. Marks upon the walls and in the floor boards indicated that at some early date the pews had been moved closer together to accommodate more communicants. With the building of a new church in the 1960s, St. Feehan's was temporarily used as a recreation facility and its pews were discarded. Those installed in St. Feehan's during its restoration at Genesee Country Village came from St. Mary's Church in Scottsville, where they were replaced by more modern (and more comfortable) seating. The pews in St. Feehan's today are those upon which its builders sat during the 1850s when they journeyed to Scottsville to attend mass, before their own church was built.

St. Feehan's Roman Catholic Church, c. 1854, from Chestnut Ridge in Chili, New York.

THE QUAKERS

By 1803 a number of members of "the Society of Religious Friends," commonly called "Quakers," arrived from New England to settle a few miles north of Canandaigua in the small community of Farmington, where they organized a "Monthly Meeting." The following year some of the Farmington Quakers moved to land just west of the Genesee River in the present Town of Wheatland, Monroe County. They were soon joined by other Quaker families from Chenango County in central New York.

The "Wheatland Meeting" was organized, and in 1825 a small frame meeting house was put up; a cobblestone meeting house followed in 1834. The Wheatland Quakers did not always dwell in perfect harmony with one another in regard to the interpretation of their beliefs. In 1854, after years of doctrinal differences, the Orthodox Quakers split away from the "Hicksites," a less fundamental group. The Hicksites stayed on in the cobblestone meeting house while the Orthodox group erected a plain one-story meeting house a few miles away. That meeting house now stands in a quiet setting at Genesee Country Village, away from the busier part of town.

The Quakers used no music in their meetings, which were given over to devout meditation. Sitting in silence, the congregation worshipped without distraction until the Divine Spirit revealed itself in one of the Friends, who would then speak out.

Pacifists now as they were then, the Genesee Country Quakers who meet annually in the old meeting house remain devoted to the basic Quaker principles of integrity and simple living.

Some buildings are simple in the extreme. Such is the one-story frame meeting house built by the Quakers on South Road in the present Town of Wheatland, Monroe County. The interior of the meeting house (which has separate entrances for men and women) was divided by partitions which could be opened or closed, depending on whether the men or women were to meet separately or together. The hard wooden benches have been reproduced from surviving examples of originals. Facing the seated congregation is a stepped platform across the front of the meeting house where the older "Friends" sat. Two stoves, two wood boxes, and two sets of shelves for books completed the interior arrangement.

The meeting house was "laid down" (to use the Quaker term) in 1873 when the size of the congregation dwindled, and the simple old structure was converted to farm use. In 1967 it was conveyed to the Museum by Mrs. Richard Field, a descendent of one of the first Wheatland Friends.

Quaker Meeting House, c. 1854, Town of Wheatland, Monroe County, New York.

The spartan interior of the circa 1854 Friends Meeting House with its hard benches.

THE SHAKERS

Until recently, the story of the Shakers in western New York—first at Sodus on Lake Ontario, then at Groveland, south of Mt. Morris—has been a little-known chapter in New York State history. A new interest in the beautifully crafted products made by Shaker hands has reawakened interest in the communal and pacifist sect.

In England in 1747, Ann Lee, young daughter of a blacksmith, was arrested with other members of the "Shaking Quakers" on charges of disturbing the Sabbath peace. While in jail, Ann had a vision that she was annointed by God to be Christ's successor. As "Mother Ann," she led her band of Believers away from their persecutors across the seas to America.

In 1776, the Shakers founded their first community at Niskayuna (now Watervliet) near Albany. There, rejecting the ideas of personal property and predestination, they followed Mother Ann's teaching: "Hands to work, hearts to God." Visitors to Shaker revival meetings spread the word, and other communities were begun throughout New England.

During the early years of the nineteenth century, the Shaker movement spread westward through upstate New York, Ohio and Kentucky. The Shakers' belief in the perfectability of man was a beacon to be followed.

In 1826, a small Shaker community was founded at Sodus, New York on a broad bay of Lake Ontario graced with rich soil and protected from unseasonable frosts. The announcement of a proposed canal through Shaker lands alarmed the Believers (who preferred to live apart from "The World") and they sold their property to the canal company in 1836.

The next year the Society purchased more than 1600 acres in the Town of Groveland in Livingston County at a site called by the Indians "Sonyea," or "The open spot where the sun shines in"—far from the worldly influences of the proposed (but never developed) canal back at Sodus.

Ironically, within a short time "The World" floated right past the Shakers on mule-hauled boats as the Genesee Valley Canal was constructed along the edge of the new colony at Sonyea.

At Sonyea, the Shakers developed a community of some thirty buildings including a meeting house, mills, shops, barns and residences. But in 1892 the Sonyea colony, reduced in numbers, closed its doors and its members moved to the Shaker community at Watervliet. The vacated property was purchased by New York State to be used as a center for the treatment of epilepsy.

In 1984, the New York State Correctional Department took over most of the old Shaker settlement, at which time Genesee Country Museum acquired the Trustees' Building.

On the first floor of the restored building a Shaker "store" has been replicated, based on illustrations accompanying nineteenth-century magazine articles about "the fascinating Shakers." Other rooms contain excellent examples of Shaker-made furniture and artifacts.

On the grounds is a vegetable garden with plants similar to those propagated by the Shakers for their seed business. A more extensive series of beds is given over to varieties of herbs grown by the Shakers when, in the middle of the nineteenth century, they were primary suppliers to American pharmaceutical firms.

These gardens are dedicated to the memory of Richard L. Turner, a founding trustee of Genesee Country Museum.

The building and its well-tended gardens serve as poignant reminders of a peaceable people and their important imprint on American culture.

The structure on the left in this old engraving of the Shaker colony at Sonyea is the Trustees' Building, one of the first to be constructed when the Shakers moved to the new site in 1837.

For half a century the wood-framed building was the headquarters and residence of the Colony's officials, both male and female.

A kitchen and dining room were on the ground floor; the top floor served as an infirmary. In the office and store on the first floor the Shakers conducted their business with "The World."

Acres of broom corn were grown, from which the famous Shaker flat brooms were made, and a thriving seed industry sent salesmen far and wide.

Shaker Trustees Building, c. 1839, from Sonyea, New York.

THE EARLY SCHOOLS

Along with their religious and civic heritages, the Genesee Country settlers brought a tradition of public education to their adopted land. The New Englanders came away from a public school development that was already a century and a half old.

The first to settle west of Canandaigua was the Adams family from New England, who in 1788 built a log house along the trail leading toward the Genesee River. James Sperry, the early settler of Ontario County, recalled that when his family arrived in the same area in 1794 there was already a school near the Adams residence, kept by Laura, one of the Adams daughters. "The next spring," Sperry recounted, "a seven by ten log schoolhouse was built one and a half miles southwest...My eldest brother and myself attended this school in the winter of '96 and '97, walking two and a half miles through the snow across the opening, not with 'old shoes and clouted' on our feet, but with rags tied on them to go and come in, taking them off in school hours."

Sperry also recalled that in 1797 "a young man with a pack on his back came into the neighborhood...and introduced himself as a school teacher from the land of steady habits; proposing that they form a new district, and he would keep their school." When his proposition was accepted he helped build another log schoolhouse. "In this school," Sperry fondly remembered, "most of us learned for the first time that the earth was round." The citizens of the district were alarmed at the news. "Although the schoolmaster was a favorite with parents and pupils, the 'most orthodox' thought that he was talking of something of which he knew nothing, and was teaching for sound doctrine what was contrary to the common sense of all; for everybody knew that the earth was flat and immovably fixed, and that the sun rose and set every day."

The author of that heresy, who went on to become Justice of the Peace, a member of the legislature, a Congressman, and moved to Brooks Grove, was Micah Brooks, who gave his name to the hamlet in Livingston County as well as the land on which was built the church now on the square at Genesee Country Village.

Not all schools and scholars were lucky enough to have uninhibited and inspiring teachers like young Micah Brooks. Most teachers were only lightly qualified, having received little if any professional training. In some instances teachers were held in low regard; in other cases they might stand next to the parson in the respect of the community.

The wages for male teachers were from eight to twenty dollars a month; for the women they were from four to ten. Teachers of either sex were boarded around the district, some getting along well enough, others nearly starving.

It was in such schoolhouses as the one-room building on the slope below the Village that a great majority of Americans received all their formal education in the early nineteenth century, not only in the Genesee Country but throughout the land. At times as many as sixty pupils crowded into a single room. A child might enter when he was three years old. By seven he was studying grammar. Then he would learn to write and how to "do sums". When he reached ten his attendance was apt to be irregular, since he was then old enough to work on the farm. In some districts there were two terms, winter and summer, the latter taught by a woman when the men were supposed to be engaged in farm work, the former term nearly always by a man.

The long benches and rude desks in the Red Schoolhouse have been reproduced in accordance with evidence found beneath overlays of wallpaper and paint on the wooden wainscot. The high homemade desk on a raised platform affords the teacher a position of authority.

Red Schoolhouse, c. 1825, from near Avon, New York.

ACADEMIES AND SEMINARIES

Books were scarce in the early years, the scholars required to provide their own. The most commonly used book — perhaps the all-time best selling (75,000,000 copies) work of any American author — was Noah Webster's spelling book, first published in 1784 and available at the bookseller's or the general store. It was the basic volume in the primary schools, in many instances the only real textbook used. This unrivalled work not only taught the young scholars how to spell and pronounce correctly but how to live virtuously, frugally, and self-reliantly.

The other tools of the trade were goosequill pens made by the teacher and ink mixed from ink powder by the teacher or by the scholars themselves. Pencils were too expensive, and steel points did not come into use until about 1830. Paper was costly and was expended sparingly. Though slates had not yet made their appearance in the early years, blackboards — boards painted black — were used by the teacher who carefully husbanded the supply of chalk.

The schoolhouses themselves left much to be desired by the teacher and the scholars but little by the taxpayers. They were overcrowded, poorly heated, poorly ventilated, poorly lighted, and poorly furnished. "They were cared for generally by all," as one writer put it, "and particularly by none." Somehow, in spite of the odds, some of the parents' hopes that their children might learn to read and spell and do sums were often fulfilled.

Some promise of relief for the sorry state of the primary schools came in 1805 when the New York State Legislature passed an act establishing a permanent fund for the support of public elementary schools. In 1812 a measure was passed providing for the establishment of school districts within the townships, for the election of local school officials, and for the distribution of state funds according to population. The towns were to raise matching money, the combined total to go for teachers' wages. Though the state funds were spread thin, they paved the way for the gradual improvement in the public school system.

The well-appointed classroom contained a piano, a drawing table, a blackboard, a wood stove, plenty of light and a well-qualified teacher.

Beginning early in the nineteenth century, private, sometimes referred to as "Select," schools for girls were established in many western New York State villages and towns, as well as in the cities. This was in part to give the girls educational opportunities equal to those offered at the boys' private academies; and in part because of the concern of church groups to provide what they considered appropriate instruction for young ladies.

The Romulus Female Seminary was built in 1855. According to town records, a subscription of some $85 dollars was collected to buy a bell "for the seminary then being built, said bell to be hung in the tower of the Seminary."

In 1883 the Seminary closed. The building was later bought by the Presbyterian Church of Romulus for use as a chapel and was moved to a site alongside the church building.

In 1970 the old Seminary building was moved once more, this time to Genesee Country Village. It has been restored and furnished as a typical girls' small seminary of the period.

Built toward the end of the Greek Revival period, the one-story building includes the basic elements of that style. Two square columns are topped by the wide entablature which, in turn, is capped by a pediment with full returns of the cornice. The iron cresting on the bell tower is of a later period, presumably added when the seminary was converted into a chapel.

Romulus Female Seminary, c. 1855, Romulus, New York.

GOVERNMENT...BY THE PEOPLE

THE TOWN HALL

The early settlers of the Genesee Country formed their churches in accordance with the established precepts of a particular denomination. However unconventional the setting—a house, a barn, an open field—the conduct of worship was generally as orthodox as circumstances allowed.

In the same way, local governments and town meetings in the newly opened land were organized along familiar lines. These civic forms did not have to evolve on the frontier. Their underlying concepts—varied according to their point of origin—were firmly fixed in the minds of the early settlers. Most newcomers to the Genesee Country expected that once the land was cleared and farms were started, when roads were improved and towns and commerce were well established, that life would become much like it had been back home—only better.

But a new kind of political awareness was about to be born on this frontier, as on other frontiers in the new nation. The first wave of settlers had been colonists, living under a king who ruled by hereditary right. Now, the Genesee Country settler had a president who was elected by representatives of the people and who ruled without any royal trappings. The new Constitutional government was by definition "of the people", and public policy was shaped by public opinion, as expressed through elected repre-sentatives. The fact that a single citizen now could play a role in the nation's decision-making process changed the political attitude of most Americans. This new sense of civic responsibility was reflected in the rapidity with which town governments were formed in the Genesee Country.

The first town meetings took place in private homes, in taverns and inns, schoolhouses, or barns. At the annual meeting, usually held the first week in April, town officials were elected, among them Supervisors, Assessors, Fence Viewers and Path-masters. Issues of public concern—schools, roads, bridges and taxes—were discussed at regularly scheduled meetings and were voted upon by eligible tax-paying voters.

As soon as the town's resources permitted and the necessary vote was taken, a town hall was built. The new addition to the community quickly became not only the seat of local government but a center for a multitude of community activities. Church groups lacking their own building held services in the town hall; singing societies and dancing classes met there; touring theatrical groups trod its boards; and patriotic celebrations centered around its hospitable presence. Many things to many people, the town hall has remained a symbol of the new nation's democratic spirit.

The Town Hall on the Village Square is an adaptation of William Hamilton's 1822 inn from South Lima, New York, as it was enlarged for public purposes. Like many early inns and taverns, Hamilton's old place hosted its share of public meetings. A tower and a clock from a Buffalo church were added when the landmark was reconstructed at the Genesee Country Village in 1980.

The Town Hall, like its early counterparts across the country, provides the setting for many of the Village activities. Perhaps the most stirring of these is the annual Fourth of July celebration held on its steps, conducted according to early Genesee Country tradition with oratory, toasts, prayers, and songs appropriate to the period. The Independence Day rites are a yearly reminder of the debt owed the heroes who guided the nation through its first years.

Town Hall, c. 1822, from South Lima, New York.

GOVERNMENT...FOR THE PEOPLE

THE POST OFFICE

Regular mail service crucial to the well-organized community did not come to the Genesee Country until roads were sufficiently improved to permit the passage of mail stages. During the first years of settlement, mail service was casual and unreliable, the mail sometimes carried by ordinary traveller and sometimes by post riders under federal contract. As the region became more accessible, postmasters were appointed to receive and distribute mail within a given locality.

Canandaigua resident Gideon Granger, Postmaster General of the United States, did much to improve mail service in his native Genesee Country.

The Brooks Grove Post Office was established by Granger in 1834. Mail reached Brooks Grove by stagecoaches plying between Mt. Morris and Nunda. During the early years service was infrequent, but it is said that on 'post day' half the village would turn out for the distribution of mail.

Postal rates in those days depended upon the distance to be covered. In 1818, a single letter delivered by one carrier travelling forty miles cost 12 cents; distance of more than 500 miles required 37½ cents postage. Frugal correspondents tried to avoid paying postage by sending letters with trustworthy travellers headed in the right direction.

Customarily the village post office was located in the general store with the storekeeper an officially appointed postmaster. Melissa Carrier, who was appointed postmistress at Brooks Grove in 1876, had difficulty getting about. Her neighbors moved her small store and post office back from the road and attached it to her dwelling—the 1835 Henry S. Jarvis House, now serving as the Parsonage near Brooks Grove Church. After nearly a century together, the buildings were separated when moved to Genesee Country Village.

Post Office, c. 1834, from Brooks Grove, New York.

The solitary post-rider carried the mail before the advent of the mail stage.

A TOWER FOR A TANNER

In 1846 Andrew Jackson Downing, architect and landscape designer of country residences and planner of the grounds of the Capitol, the White House, and the Smithsonian Institution, proclaimed: "The Greek style has passed its crisis. The people have survived it." It was true. The architectural calm which the Greek Revival had superimposed upon the American landscape was being disturbed as the "Picturesque" movement in England (a reaction against nearly two centuries of classicism in art and architecture) crossed the Atlantic, bringing with it two new vogues — the Gothic Revival and the Italianate.

Downing published books of designs for rural retreats which were adaptations of crenelated Gothic castles and the towered country villas of northern Italy. His widely read and influential works were illustrated by another architect, Alexander Jackson Davis, who became the most prolific practitioner of his time, with clients requesting designs in the Grecian, Italian, Moorish, or Gothic modes. Most of Davis's wealthy clients were ready for something more exotic than porticoes and pediments.

So was John Hamilton of Campbell, New York. Hamilton had arrived in that southern tier town in 1843 as a shoemaker; but in 1870 he was the owner of tanneries, a leading figure in his community, and the proud possessor of a grand new house.

Hamilton's towering mansion displays the full flowering of the Victorian Italianate style. The L-shaped structure, its flat pitched roof and eaves projecting outward on console-like brackets, its tall chimneys with corbelled brick mouldings, the verandas, and the bay windows all fit the Italianate formula; and the all important tower, its base embracing the paired entrance doors and its middle stories containing stairway access to the upper level, is appropriately crowned with a mansard roof.

From its dressed stone foundation walls to the iron cresting atop the tower, John Hamilton's house is every inch a fulfillment of the dictum of another influential Victorian architect, Samual Sloan, that "A man's dwelling at the present day, is not only an index of his wealth, but also of his character...and the one who builds a beautiful residence now, is as much respected as were the old Barons with their massive castles and troops of retainers."

An early photograph of the Hamilton House has made it possible to reproduce the landscape in the front of the residence as it was, with minor adjustments for the difference in setback from the road. The 'teardrop' flower beds are examples of the 'carpet bedding' which became so popular in the latter half of the nineteenth century, and are based on an illustration from Vick's Monthly Magazine, published in Rochester in 1879. The iron fence came with the house, having been dismantled some years ago and stored in the basement.

John Hamilton House, c. 1870, from Campbell, New York.

Hamilton's office and library features a many-faceted and pigeon-holed Wooten desk.

A House Not on the Square

Orson Squire Fowler, a native of the Genesee Country village of Cohocton, left his father's farm to study for the ministry at Amherst College. While at Amherst his interest switched to phrenology — that science which maintains that character and mental capacity can be analyzed by examination of the conformation of a subject's skull. With his brother and sister, Fowler published tracts extolling phrenology and clairvoyance and a diet of vegetables while warning against coffee, tea, spirits, and tightly laced dresses.

Then in 1848 Fowler published *A Home for All, or a New, Cheap, Convenient, and Superior Mode of Building* in which he announced that the octagon house with its eight sides enclosed more space than a square one with equal wall space.

"Why," asked Orson Fowler," so little progress in architecture when there is so much in other matters? Why continue to build in the same square form of all past ages?" The octagonal form had been used in public buildings in the past; but now as a concept for domestic architecture it had a dedicated and convincing champion. Fowler's books, stressing the functional and stylistic advantages of the octagon house, found many readers and several hundred followers who sprinkled the landscape from New England to Wisconsin with eight-sided houses, barns, churches, schoolhouses, carriage houses, garden houses, smokehouses, and privies.

The Gothic Revival and the Italianate expressions had not been lost upon Orson Fowler. From the Italianate he borrowed the cupolas which lighted his stairwells, the bracketed roofs, and the verandas. From the Gothic came the pointed arch windows and other embellishments in the octagon house he built for himself on a rise overlooking the Hudson River.

From various sources, including his own innovative imagination, came indoor water closets, speaking tubes, dumb waiters, hot air furnaces, hot water heaters, and ventilators. The moment of "The Home For All" was brief, although the novelty of the eight-sided building has never lost its appeal to those individuals looking for something out of the ordinary.

When Corporal Hyde returned to Friendship, New York after the Civil War, he briefly resumed farming; acquired an interest in a shingle mill; a young wife; and a new octagonal house. He and his wife shortly joined a spiritualist group.

Hyde later became a homeopathic physician. Julia, an accomplished musician and an ordained Methodist minister, held seances (it was said) in her parlor. When Julia died within two days of her husband, the belief even among sensible people arose that their departed spirits frequented the old, oddly-shaped house.

The vacant and long-neglected c. 1870 Octagon House from Friendship, Allegany County, New York, was acquired by the Museum in 1978.

One of the double parlors, furnished with Rococo Revival furniture and all the odds and ends considered essential to the well-appointed Victorian interior.

More than a dozen gardens, large and small, brighten the Museum landscape. A number are decorative accessories for the buildings and sculptures ranging around the Great Meadow. Each of the gardens within the Village, however, is designed as part of the historical environment of a particular restored building, united with it in spirit and time.

The herb gardens furnish dyes for home-woven textiles, medicines for home remedies, and condiments to enrich the flavor of foods. Of the four vegetable gardens, all organically maintained, the "Heirloom Garden" at the Jones House is of particular interest, containing only those hardy crops commonly grown in the nineteenth century kitchen garden, grown from seed "bred back" to original types.

Extensive floral gardens at two of the Village residences illustrate two distinct Genesee Country horticultural traditions.

LIVINGSTON-BACKUS GARDEN

This garden is laid out in the classical style compatible with the architecture of its Federal style garden house, built in Cortland, New York in 1826, and the residence, built in Rochester's Third Ward in the 1820s and altered to its present Greek Revival style in the 1830s.

Contemporary descriptions of several Rochester gardens of the 1830s and 40s provided the basis for the brick paths edged with boxwood and the inclusion of trees and shrubs within the flower beds. Pear was the 'cherished fruit' and often planted within the confines of the garden near the house, rather than in the orchard with the apples and cherries.

The catalogs of 1835 and 1841 of the Monroe Garden and Nursery, established by Asa Rowe in Greece, New York, provided the list of plants included in the garden. Modern perennials of the same genus and species may or may not look like those he had for sale, as many have been hybridized and improved in cultivation over the past 150 years. The roses, however, are true to their species names, and are exactly like those ancestors cultivated in the eighteenth and nineteenth centuries. All but a few bloom only once each year—in June.

The prominent men of early Rochester were avid horticulturalists, seeking out the finest and rarest plants for their gardens, and competing with each other in State Fairs for prizes in fruits and vegetables. Each plant was valued for itself and given plenty of space in the garden. Flowers were often chosen for their fragrance as well as their beauty.

The orderly arrangement of the early Rochester garden was not only appropriate from an architectural standpoint. It also served as a psychological buffer against the wilderness, which in those days lay just beyond the borders of each city lot. Only when civilization was firmly established in this region would men envision the natural world that surrounded them as romantic and picturesque. For the first settlers the virgin forest was a dismal, dark and dangerous place, an obstacle to agriculture and to their peace of mind.

The garden house, circa 1828, comes from a Cortland, New York estate. An unmatched example of the genre, its finely wrought Federal detail was achieved by woodcarver Samuel Rouse.

OCTAGON HOUSE GARDEN

The design of this garden is based on the writings of Andrew Jackson Downing, America's first landscape architect. His book, *Cottage Residences,* published in 1842, provided the form for gardens as well as the list of trees, shrubs and flowers that adorned them. Downing's writings became classics in his lifetime and brought about a profound change in the style of the American house and garden. Influenced by the writings of English and French landscapers, Downing turned against the geometrical form, advocating instead an asymetrical design, and a natural landscape which could be romantic or picturesque depending on the choice of trees and shrubs.

Downing's landscape designs called for gravel paths which meandered throughout the garden, plantings of trees and shrubs spaced so that their natural form could develop, and broad expanses of well kept lawn with numerous flower beds in flowing curves, circles and elaborate 'arabesques.' He advocated the preservation and enhancement of distant vistas, and placed a new importance on the view of the garden from the house.

Downing despised the bare earth and demanded that flowers be so thickly planted that the earth did not show. He provided detailed lists for his readers so that perennial gardens could be in a state of continuous bloom, and championed the newly introduced annual flowers such as verbenas and petunias, which could be counted on to carpet the earth with colorful blossoms for a long period.

The rising wealthy middle class of America embraced Downing's theories enthusiastically, building handsome suburban 'villas' in the variety of styles considered together as 'Victorian,' and surrounding them with elaborate landscapes. Handsome gazebos as well as rustic arbors were built in the garden for picnics and tea parties or to provide shelter in inclement weather. The study of botany became a fashionable pastime. Taking the air and communing with nature were considered essential to the health of mind, body and spirit. The useful garden of the husbandman was hidden behind fences and hedges where it could not spoil the beauty of the garden of pleasure and recreation created for the new leisure class.

A portion of the arabesques in the Octagon House Garden which are derived from designs in A.J. Downing's Cottage Residences.
In the background is a refreshment pavilion, based upon a similar structure which was destroyed by fire in Thousand Islands Park. The garden setting in the courtyard of the pavilion features a three-tiered water fountain. Lunches are served daily during the summer season.

Following Downing's dictum, paths wind about the grounds of the Octagon House. Along one of these, an eight-sided garden house provides a shady resting place. The carefully detailed structure is a replication of a rare nineteenth-century garden house ornamenting the grounds of a Victorian house in the Livingston County hamlet of Fowlerville, just a few miles from the Museum.

THE GALLERY OF SPORTING ART

Adjacent to the village site is the Gallery of Sporting Art. A collection of several hundred paintings, prints and bronze sculptures, this is the only major fine arts museum in North America specializing in sporting and wildlife art. The Gallery is the culmination of a fifty-year effort by Genesee Country Museum founder John L. Wehle, whose familiarity with wildlife—and with hunting and fishing for sport in Europe, and Africa and North America—is reflected in the international character of the art.

The visitor may divide his time among nine principal galleries, exploring the broad range of styles, settings, and artistic traditions.

BIG GAME OF NORTH AMERICA GALLERY

Among the animals depicted in their natural habitats are bighorn sheep, Rocky Mountain goats, buffalo, caribou, white-tailed deer, elk, moose, grizzly and black bear, and pronghorn antelope. Paintings by two of the twentieth-century's foremost American animal painters, Carl Rungius and Bob Kuhn, are featured.

GALLERY OF WILDLIFE WATERCOLORS

American watercolor artists, both past and present, capture field and stream landscapes of the sportsmen. Most of the artists are both sportsmen and nature lovers who have lived the life they depict. The watercolors are supplemented by an array of antique decoys—a number of them from the hands of well-known carvers.

THE GRAND GALLERY

This is a composite view of European, English and American sporting art and includes the oldest paintings in the gallery of Sporting Art collection. The sporting traditions of French noblemen, English country squires and American citizens are traced through action-packed scenes of the hunt, still-lifes of game, and portraits of sportsmen with their hounds and gun dogs.

GALLERY OF ENGLISH SPORT

The development of the Thoroughbred in eighteenth-century England and the enthusiasm for racing, and later foxhunting, gave rise to a school of sporting art in Great Britain. Paintings by some of the outstanding practitioners of the sporting genre, including John Ferneley and Henry Alken, portray fine horses and episodes from various famous hunts.

GALLERY OF "LES ANIMALIERS"

France was the birthplace of the Animalier School, which flourished from the 1830s until the turn of the century. Antoine-Louis Barye was the foremost member of "Les Animaliers," and his naturalistic animal bronzes, along with those of his followers, are well represented here as well as throughout the Gallery of Sporting Art.

AFRICAN GALLERY

While earlier artists sculpted and painted the African animals they had studied in European zoos, artists whose works are featured in the African Gallery traveled to Africa so that they could depict their wild subjects on location. Paintings by Wilhelm Kuhnert, David Shepard and Robert Bateman, and sculpture by Jonathan Kenworthy and Kenneth Bunn are supplemented by native art and artifacts.

AUDUBON/TUNNICLIFFE GALLERY

Birds are the focus of international attention here. Original engravings from Audubon's "Birds of America" are exhibited alongside watercolors by British painter Charles Tunnicliffe, Sweden's celebrated Bruno Liljefors, Canada's George McLean, New Zealand's Raymond Harris-Ching, and America's Louis Agassiz Fuertes.

TROTTING HORSE GALLERY

A change of pace is apparent in this gallery dedicated to the memory of Mr. and Mrs. Alvah G. Strong by their daughter, Marjorie Strong Wehle.

The Strongs, avid harness-horse enthusiasts, drove many of the colorful vehicles displayed here and within the Carriage Museum.

Oil paintings, sculptures, and graphics document the pageantry and excitement of the trotting horse tradition.

GALLERY OF WESTERN AMERICA

Works of some of the best-known American artists are among those displayed in the Gallery of Western America. Included are bronzes by Frederic Remington and paintings by members of the famous Taos art colony. The life of the Indian and cowboy at the turn of the century are depicted by artists who had the foresight to capture a vanishing era; and the West of today is portrayed by contemporary artists sensitive to the indigenous cultures and natural wonders of their region.

The Gallery of Sporting Art.

THE SCULPTURE GARDEN – VOICES IN BRONZE

The grounds around the Gallery of Sporting Art are punctuated by dramatic bronze sculptures – one of the largest gatherings of outdoor sculpture by American artists in the country. Some are life size, some are larger than life, and one is truly monumental.

GENESEE EAGLE

Sculptor Kent Ullberg's nine-foot high "Genesee Eagle," perched atop a twelve-foot pedestal and looking with his eagle's eye out across the Great Meadow, is perhaps the exclamation point for the powerful contemporary statements implied by those mute images.

"Until recently," said Ullberg during ceremonies at the installation of the giant bald eagle, "wildlife hasn't been glorious enough for monumental sculpture. Finally people appreciate and are concerned enough about wildlife and the environment to make public statements. Natural images are completely logical for contemporary artists."

THE UNKNOWN

Richard Greeves lives on the Wind River Indian Reservation in Wyoming. "What better place," he asks, "to study the Indian? There is magic in the Indian people who have lived and died here, and the people who live here now — my friends."

About *The Unknown* Greeves writes, "I'm sure most of us at one time have imagined what the earth must have looked like when a man was first put forth on the North American continent, and the Creator said, 'There it is, the Unknown.' "

106

CORN GRINDER

Allan Houser, a full-blooded Apache, who has been called the "Father of American Stone Carving," explains his attraction to stone. "A real sculptor hates a square block of marble. He wants the suggestion which comes from oddness; then he can work it until it's right—into a unique form." Several of Houser's marbles are displayed within the Gallery of Sporting Art.

His *Corn Grinder*, however, located just outside the Gallery entrance, is bronze. (Bronze resists exposure better than stone.) The seated metallic female figure maintains the simplicity of his stone carvings; and from it emerges the same spirit of Apache endurance.

THE GREETING

Mid-westerner George Carlson spent long periods among the Tarahumara Indians of Mexico and on reservations in the American Southwest. Carlson's reverence for the Native American Indian, his profound respect for Indian tradition, and his understanding of the quandary facing the Indian in American society are inherent in *The Greeting*. Here an Indian elder, wearing around his neck peace medals received during a visit to the American capital, extends his arm— a signal of friendship and welcome.

STRUTTING GROUNDS

Strutting Grounds comprises three finely detailed figures. A Tom turkey is performing his famous courtship ritual – tail fanned out, feathers ruffled, and wings extended to the ground – for two attentive hens. "I've always been fascinated," notes

sculptor D.H.S. Wehle (who is also a zoologist and marine biologist), "by the behavior of wildlife, whether studied within controlled conditions of the laboratory or observed over extended periods in the field."

DESCENDING COUGAR AND BOUNDING DOE

Whereas Ken Bunn's alert *Descending Cougar* is positioned to leap from his pedestal, his *Bounding Doe* is already in startled flight.

The doe, her muscles stretched, is caught for an instant in precarious balance on slender bronze forelegs.

MOUNTAIN COMRADES

Anatomical lessons from his early years as a taxidermist served Dan Ostermiller well when he later turned to sculpture. An animal watcher in both Africa and North America he hopes to make others more aware of animals and their predicaments as man invades their habitat. "By getting people emotionally involved," he believes, "their feelings will go hand-in-hand with conservation."

THE NATURE CENTER

The woodlands and old fields that border the Museum complex are home to a rich diversity of plants and wildlife, all set on the rocky landscape of the Onondaga escarpment. It is here, amongst patches of delicate ferns and massive, glacier-deposited boulders, where you will find the Genesee Country Museum's Nature Center and its four-and-a-half miles of hiking trails.

The trail system is anchored by the diverse *Perimeter Trail*, which leads the visitor to three additional trails: *Succession Trail* snakes through a grassy meadow, then an old field and finally a woodland, illustrating the natural process of succession. The beauty and abundance of a deciduous woodland is featured along the *Web of Life Trail*, a trail that is best appreciated in the spring. A temporary, woodland pond, also known as a vernal pond, is located along this trail. Here can be seen a natural bouquet of wildflowers and animals of many kinds, including the wood frog,

spotted salamander, wood duck, northern waterthrush, veery and white-tailed deer.

Geology Trail interprets the interesting geologic setting of the Nature Center. Fossilized limestone bedrock formed some 375 million years ago is visible along this trail, as is evidence of the much more recent Pleistocene glacial period. The *Lower Meadow Trail*, which loops around Bluebird Pond and a field of goldenrods and asters, is close to the Center's interpretive building and is accessible to visitors who wish a shorter walk on level ground.

Inside the interpretive building are exhibits describing the flora, fauna and geologic features of the Genesee Country. This is where visitors can closely examine ancient coral fossils or come eye to eye with amphibious pondlife. Outdoors there are several gardens featuring wildflowers native to upstate New York, as well as trees, shrubs and vines attractive to insects and songbirds.

Indigenous waterplants are displayed in a unique water garden, which includes a flowing stream.

The Nature Center staff provides educational programs throughout the year. Natural science classes are taught to area school children, and special groups often visit the Center for naturalist-guided programs. Museum visitors can participate in guided walks and other programs nearly every weekend.

Genesee Country Museum is also involved with an important wildlife management project to assist with the recovery of certain cavity-nesting birds. The eastern bluebird, which is the state bird of New York, and the wood duck have both experienced a steady and dramatic decline in population throughout much of this century. With the help of dedicated volunteers the Nature Center staff maintains nesting boxes for these and other species, and remarkable progress has been made.

This young family has discovered a bird flying through dense cover just off the Web of Life Trail.

A mother and her young daughter share the beauty of a goldenrod along the Lower Meadow Trail.

Freshly fallen leaves decorate reindeer lichen.

Bluebirds are common nesters throughout Genesee Country Museum.

THE GREAT MEADOW

On the approach to the restored Village lies a broad grassy meadow in the lea of a curving slope - a natural amphitheater for special events staged throughout the Museum season. A large gathering of Highland Bagpipers mass and march on the Meadow each spring. A nineteenth century circus comes early in the summer. The Fourth of July ceremonies and celebrations begin on the Great Meadow and end on the steps of the Town Hall in the Village; a reenactment of a Civil War begins as a skirmish in the Village and develops into a battle in the Great Meadow. A muster of horse-drawn or hand-pulled antique fire apparatus fills the Meadow with cherished and colorful machines whose owners compete in nineteenth century firemen's exercises and tests; and in the fall The Genesee Agricultural Society Fair covers a portion of the Meadow with a City of Tents, within which the poultry and animal exhibits, the displays of nineteenth century farm produce and examples of the domestic arts, the fares of vendors, the shams of sideshow men, the machinations of puppeteers blend to form the holiday scene which characterized the nineteenth century rural fair.

Surrounding the Great Meadow are The Gallery of Sporting Art, a sculpture garden, the Carriage Museum, the Education Center, the Agricultural Society's Exhibition Hall, two refreshment centers and two gift shops. In the middle of the Great Meadow a bandstand, designed after those which punctuated village squares and parks in the nineteenth century, provides a podium for band concerts of music heard in those squares and parks.

The craft and gift shop was a small station at the junction of the Buffalo, Rochester, and Pittsburgh Railroad and the Lehigh Valley Railroad a mile east of the museum site.

Centered on the great meadow is the band stand, a reproduction of an old Elmira, New York park structure.

A six horse hitch performs during the Genesee Agricultural Society Fair.

Almost all who had come to make their way in the Genesee Country expected change. They were depending upon change to remedy their various imperfect situations — economic, social, private. Once in the unsettled country and at the end of a long and unreliable supply line, the pioneers by necessity became resourceful, self-sufficient and more independent. Yet the expectations of these hardy men and women remained conditioned by their own traditions. They presumed that in a reasonable time the raw land would support better farms and more prosperous villages than those they had left; that the familiar institutions which had ordered their former communities would be reestablished to stabilize the new settlements. But none of the pioneers could foresee all that lay ahead in the Genesee Country.

Not even visionaries like Charles Williamson, late of the British army, nor an optimistic and large scale landowner like James Wadsworth of Connecticut, nor enterprising men like Nathaniel Rochester from Virginia could forecast the vital and dynamic alterations which would come about during the growing years of the Republic. Though they had seen a political revolution, they had witnessed no startling technological changes and, therefore, anticipated none.

These leaders and the men whom they led were still travelling by horse or in horse-drawn vehicles in much the same manner as Julius Caesar and Charlemagne. Buildings were heated, as they had been for centuries, by fireplaces. Candles provided illumination. The land was worked and its crops harvested in ways little changed from the Middle Ages. Farm animal husbandry was carried on much as it always had been. All these aspects of working and living were to change dramatically.

The first great change in the Genesee Country came with the completion of the Erie Canal in 1825. Canals, where heavy loads could be carried on barges, were being used successfully in the East. But those canals were short and confined to the flat coastal plain. Thomas Jefferson declared that "talk of making a canal three hundred and fifty miles through the wilderness — it is a little short of madness."

Madness or not, thanks to the advocacy of Governor DeWitt Clinton, the waterway between the Hudson River and Lake Erie was completed in eight years and was an immediate success. Trade and commerce flourished along its entire route. Towns alongside the canal swelled into important cities. The effect of the Erie Canal upon the economy of the Genesee Country was sweeping, days not weeks now separating Genesee Country flour from New York City and its harbour.

Freight was carried on the canal at one twentieth the cost of moving it overland.

The Genesee farmer who had not long since burned timber and boiled the ashes to produce a one-time crop was now prospering — sowing and harvesting wheat on a biannual basis, and selling all he could bring forth. This happy situation would prevail for a quarter of a century before competition from larger scale wheat growers in the West and the wheat "midge" of the 1850s forced a decline in wheat production within the Genesee Country.

Westward on the busy waterway came products from the rapidly industrializing East: cast iron stoves and fences from the foundries; tools and utensils from machine shops and manufacturing plants; cotton and woolen goods from textile mills; carpets and wallpapers in the latest fashion to add comfort and color to Genesee Country dwellings; oil lamps, china, and glass for convenience and for nice; and, in 1840 the *Young Lion,* the first locomotive for the Auburn and Rochester Railroad. The boatmen who delivered the locomotive to Rochester surely failed to recognize the irony of their aiding and abetting an all-weather rival which would soon threaten their own enterprise with obsolescence.

The railroad brought another great change in the affairs of the Genesee Country, with the network of lines which by 1860 extended rail service throughout the region. The flow of commerce was no longer limited to the canals and main highways. At the same time, local steam-powered industries had begun to supply many of the products formerly imported from the East. Mechanical reapers eased life for the farmer, and labor saving devices removed much of the drudgery from other work activities — both on the farm and in the home.

The Civil War, as had other wars before it, accelerated change —bringing about more mechanization on the farm and additional industries in the cities and towns. As America headed for its centennial year, the Genesee Country underwent further changes in its face and character. Its people, slowly recovering from the shock of the war, suffered new disruptions and anxiety occasioned by the Panic of 1873. There was a greater infusion of immigrants from Europe, most of whom headed for jobs in the larger communities. As the farms were forced to adopt new crop and livestock patterns, they increased in size and decreased in number. Capital was drained from the country to the city. Also to the city from the hinterlands was the steadily growing flow of the sons and daughters of the Genesee Country.

ACKNOWLEDGEMENTS AND SOURCES

Many persons in many different ways have helped make this account of the Genesee Country Museum possible. Their generous contribution of time, care, hard work, and professional attention is gratefully acknowledged:

John Adams
Scott Adamson
Daniel Barber
Cheryl Barney
Peggy Beach
Robert Becker
Lynn Belluscio
Jo Betz
Robin Blair
Robert Blaker
Todd Brady
Stephen Clary
John Danicic
Harwood Dryer
Ruby Foote
Charles Harkins
Charles Hayes
Doris Hoot
Diane Jones
Susan Kennedy
William King
Suzanne Koch
John Lurz
Malcom MacPherson
Ethel Jane Martin
Blake McKelvey
Rev. Robert F. McNamara
Ruby Mitchell
Rev. Donald J. Murphy
Kay Prey
Ann Salter
Carl Schmitt
Victoria Schmitt
Marguerite Sharp
William Siles
J. Holman Swinney
Robert VanHoute
Patricia Way
Jessie Woodward
Marjorie Strong Wehle
John L. Wehle
John L. Wehle, Jr.

Beers, F.W., *History of Allegany County, New York*. New York, 1879.

Beers, F.W., *History of Monroe County, New York*. New York.

Bigelow, Timothy. *Journal of a Tour to Niagara Falls in 1805*. Boston, 1876

Campbell, Patrick. *Travels in the Interior Inhabited Parts of North American in the Years 1791 and 1792*. Edinburgh, 1793.

Clayton, W.W., *History of Steuben County, New York*. Philadelphia, 1879.

Doty, Lockwood L., *A History of Livingston County, New York*. Geneseo, 1876.

Doty, Lockwood R., ed., *History of the Genesee Country, New York*. Chicago, 1925.

Downing, A.J., *The Architecture of Country Houses*. New York, 1850.

Fowler, Orson S., *The Octagon House, A Home For All*. (Dover ed.) New York, 1973.

Hedrick, Ulysses D., *A History of Agriculture in the State of New York*. Albany, 1935

Hunt, Gaillard. *Life in America One Hundred Years Ago*. New York, 1914.

La Rochefoucauld-Liancourt. *Travels Through the United States of America, the Country of the Iroquois and Upper Canada in the Years 1795, 1796 and 1797*. London, 1799.

Mau, Clayton. *The Development of Central and Western New York*. Dansville, 1958.

McKelvey, Blake. *Rochester, the Water Power City, 1812-1854*. Cambridge, Mass., 1945.

McKelvey, Blake. ed., *Foreign Traveler's Notes on Rochester and the Genesee Country Before 1840*. Rochester, 1940.

McNall, Neil Adams. *An Agricultural History of the Genesee Valley*. Philadelphia, 1952

Moore, D.D.T., pub., *Moore's Rural New Yorker*. Rochester, 1851-1855.

Munro, Robert. *A Description of the Genesee Country in the State of New York*. New York, 1804.

O'Callaghan, E.B., *The Documentary History of New York*. Vols. II, III. Albany, 1849.

O'Reilly, Henry. *Sketches of Rochester*. Rochester, 1838.

Parker, Arthur C., *Charles Williamson — Builder of the Genesee Country*. Rochester, 1927.

Parker, Arthur C., *The Natural Forces that Molded the Genesee Country*. Rochester, 1923.

Parker, Arthur C., *The Red Man's Gateway of the Genesee Country*. Rochester, 1927.

Percival, J., pub., *The Livingston Register*. Vol. II, No. 63. Geneseo, 1825.

Pickering, Ernest. *The Homes of America*. New York, 1951.

Ripley, H., pub., *The Moscow Advertiser*. Vol. IV, No. 186. Moscow, New York, 1820.

Rochester Museum and Science Center, pub., *Clay in the Hands of the Potter*. Rochester, 1974.

Schmidt, Carl F., *History of the Town of Wheatland*. Scottsville, 1954.

Schmidt, Carl F., *The Victorian Era in the United States*. Scottsville, 1971.

Sloan, Samuel. *The Model Architect*. Philadelphia, 1852.

Slocum, George R., *Wheatland, Monroe County, New York*. Scottsville, 1908.

Smith, James H., *History of Livingston County, New York*. Syracuse, 1881.

Spafford, Horatio G., *A Gazeteer of the State of New York*. Albany 1813.

Tucker, Luther. ed., *The Genesee Farmer*. Rochester 1831-1838.

Turner, Orsamus. *History of the Holland Purchase*. Buffalo, 1848.

Turner, Orsamus. *History of the Pioneer Settlement of the Phelps and Gorham Purchase*. Rochester, 1851.

VanWagenen, Jared. *The Golden Age of Homespun*. Albany, 1927.

Webster, Noah. *The American Dictionary of the English Language*. Boston, 1828.

Artistic Direction: Bonnie Gisel and Stephen Soeffing. Photography: John Danicic, Ruby Foote, J.D. Small, and Gary Whelpley. Editorial Consultant: Nancy Bolger.

The Genesee Country Museum was conceived and founded by John L. Wehle who from its inception has served as Chairman of the Board of Trustees. An avid outdoorsman and lifetime collector of sporting art, Jack Wehle perceived that another art form — the work of regional carpenters,

John L. Wehle

master builders, and housewrights — was fast disappearing from the landscape, and with it was vanishing an important aspect of the Genesee Valley heritage. He envisioned a museum village of selected examples of nineteenth century Genesee Country architecture.

By the early 1960s a gallery in which to share with the public his ever-growing collection of sporting art was also taking shape in Wehle's mind. These two purposes began to take tangible form in 1966 when the Genesee Country Museum was chartered by the Board of Regents of the State of New York and the first fine old building was moved to the museum site on a quiet hillside in rural Monroe County. Ten years later the museum was opened to the public in honor of the nation's Bicentennial.

Born and raised in Rochester, New York, Wehle attended Yale University and the University of Rochester. In 1945 he became president of the family business, the Genesee Brewing Company of Rochester; today he serves as Chairman of the Board.

When he was five years old, Stuart Bolger inherited from an uncle a box of pressed ceramic Anchor Blocks in good condition. With these he could construct a simple stone cottage. Under the Christmas tree in 1928 was a package containing enough Lincoln Logs to build a cabin, a barn, and some log fences.

Stuart Bolger

But the real building boom occurred with the arrival on College Hill in Elmira, New York, of a new kid on the block who brought with him an unlimited supply of hardwood building blocks. Whole villages could now be created.

It was not until 1966 with the founding of the Genesee Country Museum that this early apprenticeship could be turned to its full advantage — in bringing together disparate parts to form a "village that might have been" based on well-researched historical precedents. Between early inspiration and practical application Bolger had earned a degree in the History of Art at the University of Rochester and had served in the Marine Corps in the Pacific during World War II. Graduate studies in architectural history at Harvard and eight years directing restoration of 18th c. Moravian buildings in Bethlehem, Pa. further prepared him for the quarter of a century he has devoted to the development of Genesee Country Museum.

"Men make houses but women make homes." This reminder from *Poor Richard's Almanac* suggests in part the role Chief Curator Doris Hoot has played in the development of the Genesee Country Museum. As men brought in and restored the buildings which other men before them a century or

Doris Hoot

more ago had built, she undertook the task of turning the empty houses into the homes made by women before her — a century or more ago.

A Phi Beta Kappa graduate of the University of Rochester, Doris Hoot applied her scholarly habits toward an understanding of the circumstances, time, and place of each building.

Doris Hoot has established and meticulously maintained a concern for the proper care of the thousands of items in the museum's collections — from pin cushions to pianos; from needlepoint pillows to portrait paintings. She has provided carefully researched backgrounds and documentation for the interpretation of the furnished buildings; and she refines and retunes the settings whenever prompted by new findings concerning the lives of the men who built the houses and the women who made them into homes.

OF HILLS AND SUMMITS

Gannett Hill stands in the heart of Genesee Country—the highest point of the Bristol Hills. In a farmhouse there in 1876 was born someone who would reach a summit in the history of the American newspaper.

The farm fared badly, and before long the Gannetts set off on a quest for better times. In the hardscrabble environment of the Upper Genesee, things didn't come easily. But Maria Brooks Gannett, a hard-working and hopeful woman, often repeated her charge to her son Frank to "be somebody," and at an early age Frank Ernest Gannett set about to make his own way.

Keeping up his studies and working at odd jobs, he prepared himself for and put himself through Cornell University. Upon graduation in 1898, he signed on as a reporter with the Syracuse *Herald* at $15 a week.

Gannett became a partner in the Elmira, N.Y. *Gazette* in 1906 and continued as a part owner when a 1907 merger created the *Star-Gazette*. A believer that newspapers should have political, financial and local autonomy, he put his independent editorial philosophy into effect in his role as a managing editor for news and editorials.

The partnership went on to acquire the *Ithaca Journal*, buy and merge the Rochester *Union and Advertiser* and the *Times* into the *Times-Union* in 1918, and purchase the Utica *Observer* and the *Herald-Dispatch*, merging them into the *Observer-Dispatch* in 1921. In 1923, Elmira's two morning papers, the *Advertiser* and the *Telegram*, were added to what became known as the Empire State Group.

In 1924, Frank Gannett took the offered opportunity to become sole owner of the six newspapers. He formed Gannett Co., Inc., called his papers the Gannett Newspaper Group, and continued to increase his holdings through the purchase of papers in eleven New York State cities and in several other states.

To insure that his independent editorial policies would continue at his newspapers after his death, Gannett created the Frank E. Gannett Newspaper Foundation with a gift of stock in 1935. In his will, he directed that foundation officers "should do their utmost at all times to maintain the freedom of the press, freedom of speech and

freedom of religious worship—the most precious heritage we enjoy."

In 1991, the Gannett Foundation was renamed The Freedom Forum. Its original endowment has grown to over $715 million in diversified, managed assets, placing it at the top of the nation's media-oriented foundations. In accord with Frank Gannett's wishes, The Freedom Forum is dedicated to free press, free speech and free spirit, and is:

- a promoter of First Amendment freedoms;
- a major supporter of journalism education;
- a leader in providing professional development of journalists;
- a champion of minority and female advancement in news-media professions;
- a growing force in international freedom programs.

Today, from its World Center Headquarters, The Freedom Forum coordinates and conducts national and international initiatives to promote its priorities. The Freedom Forum's main operating programs are The Freedom Forum Media Studies Center, at Columbia University in New York City; and The Freedom Forum First Amendment Center, at Vanderbilt University in Nashville, Tenn.

The printing of this book was made possible by a grant from The Freedom Forum.